D1233362

COMPULSIVE BEHAVIOR

GENERAL EDITORS

Dale C. Garell, M.D.
Medical Director, California Children Services, Department of Health Services,
   County of Los Angeles
Associate Dean for Curriculum; Clinical Professor, Department of Pediatrics &
   Family Medicine, University of Southern California School of Medicine
Former President, Society for Adolescent Medicine

Solomon H. Snyder, M.D.
Distinguished Service Professor of Neuroscience, Pharmacology, and Psychiatry,
   Johns Hopkins University School of Medicine
Former President, Society for Neuroscience
Albert Lasker Award in Medical Research, 1978

CONSULTING EDITORS

Robert W. Blum, M.D., Ph.D.
Professor and Director, Division of General Pediatrics and Adolescent Health,
   University of Minnesota

Charles E. Irwin, Jr., M.D.
Professor of Pediatrics; Director, Division of Adolescent Medicine, University of
   California, San Francisco

Lloyd J. Kolbe, Ph.D.
Director of the Division of Adolescent and School Health, Center for Chronic
   Disease Prevention and Health Promotion, Centers for Disease Control

Jordan J. Popkin
Former Director, Division of Federal Employee Occupational Health, U.S. Public
   Health Service Region I

Joseph L. Rauh, M.D.
Professor of Pediatrics and Medicine, Adolescent Medicine, Children's Hospital
   Medical Center, Cincinnati
Former President, Society for Adolescent Medicine

THE ENCYCLOPEDIA OF
HEALTH

PSYCHOLOGICAL DISORDERS
AND THEIR TREATMENT

Solomon H. Snyder, M.D. · General Editor

COMPULSIVE
BEHAVIOR

Richard Sebastian

Introduction by C. Everett Koop, M.D., Sc.D.

former Surgeon General, U. S. Public Health Service

CHELSEA HOUSE PUBLISHERS

New York · Philadelphia

The goal of the ENCYCLOPEDIA OF HEALTH *is to provide general information in the ever-changing areas of physiology, psychology, and related medical issues. The titles in this series are not intended to take the place of the professional advice of a physician or other health care professional.*

ON THE COVER Lady Macbeth, wife of the Scotch laird in Shakespeare's great drama *Macbeth*, walks in her sleep while compulsively rubbing her hands to rid them of the imaginary blood of Duncan, king of Scotland, whom Macbeth has murdered in a plot devised by her and her husband.

CHELSEA HOUSE PUBLISHERS
EDITOR-IN-CHIEF   Richard S. Papale
EXECUTIVE MANAGING EDITOR   Karyn Gullen Browne
COPY CHIEF   Philip Koslow
PICTURE EDITOR   Adrian G. Allen
ART DIRECTOR   Nora Wertz
MANUFACTURING DIRECTOR   Gerald Levine
SYSTEMS MANAGER   Lindsey Ottman
PRODUCTION COORDINATOR   Marie Claire Cebrián-Ume

The Encyclopedia of Health
SENIOR EDITOR   Kenneth W. Lane

Staff for COMPULSIVE BEHAVIOR
COPY EDITOR   Margaret Dornfeld
EDITORIAL ASSISTANT   Laura Petermann
PICTURE RESEARCHER   Sandy Jones
DESIGNER   Robert Yaffe

3 5 7 9 8 6 4 2

Library of Congress Cataloging-in-Publication Data

Sebastian, Richard.
   Compulsive behavior/by Richard Sebastian; introduction by C. Everett Koop.
      p. cm.—(The Encyclopedia of health)
   Includes bibliographical references and index.
   Summary: An examination of compulsive behavior, focusing on the causes, effects, and treatment of this disorder.
   ISBN 0-7910-0044-3
        0-7910-0510-0 (pbk.)
   1. Obsessive-compulsive disorder—Juvenile literature. [1. Obsessive-compulsive disorder.] I. Title. II. Series.
RC533.G58 1993   92-16053
616.85'227—dc20   CIP
                                                                                        AC

CONTENTS

THE ENCYCLOPEDIA OF
H E A L T H

THE HEALTHY BODY

The Circulatory System
Dental Health
The Digestive System
The Endocrine System
Exercise
Genetics & Heredity
The Human Body: An Overview
Hygiene
The Immune System
Memory & Learning
The Musculoskeletal System
The Nervous System
Nutrition
The Reproductive System
The Respiratory System
The Senses
Sleep
Speech & Hearing
Sports Medicine
Vision
Vitamins & Minerals

THE LIFE CYCLE

Adolescence
Adulthood
Aging
Childhood
Death & Dying
The Family
Friendship & Love
Pregnancy & Birth

MEDICAL ISSUES

Careers in Health Care
Environmental Health
Folk Medicine
Health Care Delivery
Holistic Medicine
Medical Ethics
Medical Fakes & Frauds
Medical Technology
Medicine & the Law
Occupational Health
Public Health

PSYCHOLOGICAL DISORDERS AND THEIR TREATMENT

Anxiety & Phobias
Child Abuse
Compulsive Behavior
Delinquency & Criminal Behavior
Depression
Diagnosing & Treating Mental Illness
Eating Habits & Disorders
Learning Disabilities
Mental Retardation
Personality Disorders
Schizophrenia
Stress Management
Suicide

MEDICAL DISORDERS AND THEIR TREATMENT

AIDS
Allergies
Alzheimer's Disease
Arthritis
Birth Defects
Cancer
The Common Cold
Diabetes
Emergency Medicine
Gynecological Disorders
Headaches
The Hospital
Kidney Disorders
Medical Diagnosis
The Mind-Body Connection
Mononucleosis and Other Infectious Diseases
Nuclear Medicine
Organ Transplants
Pain
Physical Handicaps
Poisons & Toxins
Prescription & OTC Drugs
Sexually Transmitted Diseases
Skin Disorders
Stroke & Heart Disease
Substance Abuse
Tropical Medicine

PREVENTION
AND
EDUCATION:
THE KEYS
TO GOOD HEALTH

C. Everett Koop, M.D., Sc.D.
former Surgeon General,
U.S. Public Health Service

The issue of health education has received particular attention in recent years because of the presence of AIDS in the news. But our response to this particular tragedy points up a number of broader issues that doctors, public health officials, educators, and the public face. In particular, it points up the necessity for sound health education for citizens of all ages.

Over the past 25 years this country has been able to bring about dramatic declines in the death rates for heart disease, stroke, accidents, and for people under the age of 45, cancer. Today, Americans generally eat better and take better care of themselves than ever before. Thus, with the help of modern science and technology, they have a better chance of surviving serious—even catastrophic—illnesses. That's the good news.

But, like every phonograph record, there's a flip side, and one with special significance for young adults. According to a report issued in 1979 by Dr. Julius Richmond, my predecessor as Surgeon General, Americans aged 15 to 24 had a higher death rate in 1979 than they did 20 years earlier. The causes: violent death and injury, alcohol and drug abuse, unwanted pregnancies, and sexually transmitted diseases. Adolescents are particularly vulnerable because they are beginning to explore their own sexuality and perhaps to experiment with drugs. The need for educating young people is critical, and the price of neglect is high.

Yet even for the population as a whole, our health is still far from what it could be. Why? A 1974 Canadian government report attributed all death and disease to four broad elements: inadequacies in the health care system, behavioral factors or unhealthy life-styles, environmental hazards, and human biological factors.

To be sure, there are diseases that are still beyond the control of even our advanced medical knowledge and techniques. And despite yearnings that are as old as the human race itself, there is no "fountain of youth" to ward off aging and death. Still, there is a solution to many of the problems that undermine sound health. In a word, that solution is prevention. Prevention, which includes health promotion and education, saves lives, improves the quality of life, and in the long run, saves money.

In the United States, organized public health activities and preventive medicine have a long history. Important milestones in this country or foreign breakthroughs adopted in the United States include the improvement of sanitary procedures and the development of pasteurized milk in the late 19th century and the introduction in the mid-20th century of effective vaccines against polio, measles, German measles, mumps, and other once-rampant diseases. Internationally, organized public health efforts began on a wide-scale basis with the International Sanitary Conference of 1851, to which 12 nations sent representatives. The World Health Organization, founded in 1948, continues these efforts under the aegis of the United Nations, with particular emphasis on combating communicable diseases and the training of health care workers.

Despite these accomplishments, much remains to be done in the field of prevention. For too long, we have had a medical care system that is science- and technology-based, focused, essentially, on illness and mortality. It is now patently obvious that both the social and the economic costs of such a system are becoming insupportable.

Implementing prevention—and its corollaries, health education and promotion—is the job of several groups of people.

First, the medical and scientific professions need to continue basic scientific research, and here we are making considerable progress. But increased concern with prevention will also have a decided impact on how primary care doctors practice medicine. With a shift to health-based rather than morbidity-based medicine, the role of the "new physician" will include a healthy dose of patient education.

Second, practitioners of the social and behavioral sciences—psychologists, economists, city planners—along with lawyers, business leaders, and government officials—must solve the practical and ethical dilemmas confronting us: poverty, crime, civil rights, literacy, education, employment, housing, sanitation, environmental protection, health care delivery systems, and so forth. All of these issues affect public health.

Third is the public at large. We'll consider that very important group in a moment.

Fourth, and the linchpin in this effort, is the public health profession—doctors, epidemiologists, teachers—who must harness the professional expertise of the first two groups and the common sense and cooperation of the third, the public. They must define the problems statistically and qualitatively and then help us set priorities for finding the solutions.

To a very large extent, improving those statistics is the responsibility of every individual. So let's consider more specifically what the role of the individual should be and why health education is so important to that role. First, and most obvious, individuals can protect themselves from illness and injury and thus minimize their need for professional medical care. They can eat nutritious food; get adequate exercise; avoid tobacco, alcohol, and drugs; and take prudent steps to avoid accidents. The proverbial "apple a day keeps the doctor away" is not so far from the truth, after all.

Second, individuals should actively participate in their own medical care. They should schedule regular medical and dental checkups. Should they develop an illness or injury, they should know when to treat themselves and when to seek professional help. To gain the maximum benefit from any medical treatment that they do require, individuals must become partners in that treatment. For instance, they should understand the effects and side effects of medications. I counsel young physicians that there is no such thing as too much information when talking with patients. But the corollary is the patient must know enough about the nuts and bolts of the healing process to understand what the doctor is telling him or her. That is at least partially the patient's responsibility.

Education is equally necessary for us to understand the ethical and public policy issues in health care today. Sometimes individuals will encounter these issues in making decisions about their own treatment or that of family members. Other citizens may encounter them as jurors in medical malpractice cases. But we all become involved, indirectly, when we elect our public officials, from school board members to the president. Should surrogate parenting be legal? To what extent is drug testing desirable, legal, or necessary? Should there be public funding for family planning, hospitals, various types of medical research, and other medical care for the indigent? How should we allocate scant technological resources, such as kidney dialysis and organ transplants? What is the proper role of government in protecting the rights of patients?

What are the broad goals of public health in the United States today? In 1980, the Public Health Service issued a report aptly entitled *Promoting Health—Preventing Disease: Objectives for the Nation*. This report expressed its goals in terms of mortality and in terms of intermediate goals in education and health improvement. It identified 15 major concerns: controlling high blood pressure; improving family planning; improving pregnancy care and infant health; increasing the rate of immunization; controlling sexually transmitted diseases; controlling the presence of toxic agents and radiation in the environment; improving occupational safety and health; preventing accidents; promoting water fluoridation and dental health; controlling infectious diseases; decreasing smoking; decreasing alcohol and drug abuse; improving nutrition; promoting physical fitness and exercise; and controlling stress and violent behavior.

For healthy adolescents and young adults (ages 15 to 24), the specific goal was a 20% reduction in deaths, with a special focus on motor vehicle injuries and alcohol and drug abuse. For adults (ages 25 to 64), the aim was 25% fewer deaths, with a concentration on heart attacks, strokes, and cancers.

Smoking is perhaps the best example of how individual behavior can have a direct impact on health. Today, cigarette smoking is recognized as the single most important preventable cause of death in our society. It is responsible for more cancers and more cancer deaths than any other known agent; is a prime risk factor for heart and blood vessel disease, chronic bronchitis, and emphysema; and is a frequent cause of complications in pregnancies and of babies born prematurely, underweight, or with potentially fatal respiratory and cardiovascular problems.

Since the release of the Surgeon General's first report on smoking in 1964, the proportion of adult smokers has declined substantially, from 43% in 1965 to 30.5% in 1985. Since 1965, 37 million people have quit smoking. Although there is still much work to be done if we are to become a "smoke-free society," it is heartening to note that public health and public education efforts—such as warnings on cigarette packages and bans on broadcast advertising—have already had significant effects.

In 1835, Alexis de Tocqueville, a French visitor to America, wrote, "In America the passion for physical well-being is general." Today, as then, health and fitness are front-page items. But with the greater scientific and technological resources now available to us, we are in a far stronger position to make good health care available to everyone. And with the greater technological threats to us as we approach the 21st century, the need to do so is more urgent than ever before. Comprehensive information about basic biology, preventive medicine, medical and surgical treatments, and related ethical and public policy issues can help you arm yourself with the knowledge you need to be healthy throughout your life.

FOREWORD

Solomon H. Snyder, M.D.

Mental disorders represent the number one health problem for the United States and probably for the entire human population. Some studies estimate that approximately one-third of all Americans suffer from some sort of emotional disturbance. Depression of varying severity will affect as many as 20% of all of us at one time or another in our lives. Severe anxiety is even more common.

Adolescence is a time of particular susceptibility to emotional problems. Teenagers are undergoing significant changes in their brain as well as their physical structure. The hormones that alter the organs of reproduction during puberty also influence the way we think and feel. At a purely psychological level, adolescents must cope with major upheavals in their lives. After years of not noticing the opposite sex, they find themselves romantically attracted but must painfully learn the skills of social interchange both for superficial, flirtatious relationships and for genuine intimacy. Teenagers must develop new ways of relating to their parents. Adolescents strive for independence. Yet, our society is structured in such a way that teenagers must remain dependent on their parents for many more years. During adolescence, young men and women examine their own intellectual bents and begin to plan the type of higher education and vocation they believe they will find most fulfilling.

Because of these challenges, teenagers are more emotionally volatile than adults. Passages from extreme exuberance to dejection are common. The emotional distress of completely normal adolescence can be so severe that the same disability in an adult would be labeled as major mental illness. Although most teenagers somehow muddle through and emerge unscathed, a number of problems are more frequent among adolescents than among adults. Many psychological aberrations reflect severe disturbances, although these are sometimes not regarded as "psychiatric." Eating disorders, to which young adults are especially vulnerable, are an example. An extremely large number of teenagers diet to great excess even though they are not overweight. Many of them suffer from a specific disturbance referred to as anorexia nervosa, a form of self-starvation that is just as real a disorder as diabetes. The same is true for those who eat compulsively and then sometimes force themselves to vomit. They may be afflicted with bulimia.

Depression is also surprisingly frequent among adolescents, although its symptoms may be less obvious in young people than they are in adults. And, because suicide occurs most frequently in those suffering from depression, we must be on the lookout for subtle hints of despondency in those close to us. This is especially urgent because teenage suicide is a rapidly worsening national problem.

The volumes on Psychological Disorders and Their Treatment in the ENCYCLOPEDIA OF HEALTH cover the major areas of mental illness, from mild to severe. They also emphasize the means available for getting help. *Anxiety and Phobias, Depression,* and *Schizophrenia* deal specifically with these forms of mental disturbance. *Child Abuse* and *Delinquency and Criminal Behavior* explore abnormalities of behavior that may stem from environmental and social influences as much as from biological or psychological illness. *Personality Disorders* and *Compulsive Behavior* explain how people develop disturbances of their overall personality. *Learning Disabilities* investigates disturbances of the mind that may reflect neurological derangements as much as psychological abnormalities. *Mental Retardation* explains the various causes of this many-sided handicap, including the genetic component, complications during pregnancy, and traumas during birth. *Suicide* discusses the epidemiology of this tragic phenomenon and outlines the assistance available to those who are at risk. *Stress Management* locates the source of stress in contemporary society and considers formal strategies for coping with it. Finally, *Diagnosing and Treating Mental Illness* explains to the reader how professionals sift through various signs and symptoms to define the exact nature of the various mental disorders and fully describes the most effective means of alleviating them.

Fortunately, when it comes to psychological disorders, knowing the facts is a giant step toward solving the problems.

CHAPTER 1

DEFINING COMPULSIVE BEHAVIOR

Although we may speak of a person's "obsession" with the stock market or "compulsion" to eat, our everyday understanding of these terms differs markedly from the condition known as obsessive-compulsive disorder.

Alan was in many ways a normal boy. Yet even as a toddler, he had been fussy about keeping his things in order, and didn't want other people coming into his room and touching them. As he grew older, his need to have everything around him in "perfect" order extended beyond his room to encompass his entire home. By the time he was 14, his compulsive cleaning and arranging of objects was consuming large amounts of time, affecting his grades in school, and disturbing his family.

He could not bear to see smudges on mirrors, glass doors, or other smooth surfaces such as those of the refrigerator or microwave oven. If he found a smudge, he would immediately get a paper towel and bottle of spray cleaner and clean it off. He avoided going into parts of his house in which he might feel this irresistible urge to clean.

Alan also felt impelled to arrange the shoes and hangers in everyone's closets so that they were all exactly one inch apart. At times his father had to drag him bodily out of a closet where he was arranging shoes and bring him to the dinner table so that he could eat with everybody else. He arranged the contents of all the drawers in the house so that the clothes were lined up and symmetrical. Magazines and books lying on a table had to be lined up with their edges parallel to the table edge. Alan also arranged furniture in parallel or symmetrical lines; he would jockey the kitchen chairs around until he got them into positions that felt "right" to him.

When Alan closed a door, he had to check it three times to be sure that it really was closed. In school he tried to write perfectly without mistakes, but if he misspelled a word, he would stop and begin the entire assignment over again. When he closed a door, washed his hands, and brushed his teeth, he had the need to count.

When he didn't perform these rituals, or when someone in his family would touch something he had arranged, Alan would feel unbearably anxious. His behavior led to arguments with other family members.

His mother felt that she should be able to control his behavior, while his father became angry at it, causing major confrontations.

In fact, Alan himself did not enjoy any of his actions and was very unhappy about his behavior. His counting, cleaning, and arranging embarrassed him, and because his need to perform these activities was largely evoked by objects in his home, he avoided inviting other children to his house. Although people at school noticed the perfect arrangement of the things in Alan's room and his problems with writing, they shrugged these off by assuming he was a perfectionist. Other than hiding his problem, Alan did not know there was anything he could do about it.

By the time he entered ninth grade, Alan's rituals were taking up so much time that his parents took him to a psychiatrist, who diagnosed him as having *obsessive-compulsive disorder (OCD)*.

OCD, a psychological disorder typically marked by uncontrollable, repeated thoughts and recurrent, "driven" patterns of ritual-like behavior, has only recently been recognized as far more common than previously believed. It often begins in childhood, with parents often mistaking its behavior patterns for willfully bad behavior and so punishing their child, or assuming that the child will eventually outgrow the behavior. Some children manage to hide the disorder even from both their parents and their friends.

Today, however, both the scientific understanding and public awareness of OCD are growing. People who have for years suffered its burden in secret are seeking relief from it, and a growing number of effective treatments are available to them.

In Alan's case, the psychiatrist outlined various drug therapies that could be used to treat him and described another technique, not involving drugs, known as behavioral therapy. Alan's parents chose the latter and were referred to a psychologist who offered this form of treatment.

As a first step, the psychologist asked Alan to list the various situations that evoked his ritualized behaviors and asked him to rate them in terms of how anxious each would make him if he did not perform his ritual behavior in response to the situation. Each week, Alan got a "homework" assignment that involved his entering a particular situation, beginning with the least anxiety-provoking situations first, and resisting his compulsive response to it.

Although he was at first reluctant to even admit to the therapist that he had these rituals, Alan worked diligently at these assignments once he realized there was actually something he could do to get rid of them. Within four months he was free of his symptoms without needing to take any drugs. What was more, he had learned a technique called response prevention that he could use in the future to treat himself if his need to perform his rituals recurred.

Unlike Alan, who was particularly fortunate in being able to relieve his symptoms with only a short course in behavioral therapy, the majority of obsessive-compulsives do need to take drugs and may never be entirely free of symptoms.

Nevertheless, most of them can lead normal, productive lives and avoid the stigma of thinking—and having others think—that they are "crazy." In fact, some researchers now believe that OCD is caused by a chemical disorder of the brain. It is not the patient's own "fault," nor is it caused by poor upbringing.

What Is OCD?

People commonly talk about themselves or others as being "obsessive" or "compulsive." They may say a woman is "obsessed" with a man she is in love with or describe a man who is very neat, always punctual, and works all the time without ever having fun as being "compulsive." Similarly, excessive eating, drinking, sexual behavior, and gambling are also referred to as compulsive behaviors.

When used in reference to OCD, however, the terms *obsession* and *compulsion* have very specific meanings. *Obsessions* are persistent thoughts, images, impulses, or ideas that keep running through a person's mind even though they are meaningless and unwanted. Often these thoughts focus on unpleasant or even repulsive themes. They may take the form of incessant worry about becoming dirty or contaminated, or the fear of having an uncontrollable impulse to hurt or kill a loved one, or the fear that a fire, automobile accident, or other disaster will occur.

Compulsions are urges to perform certain behaviors in response to these obsessions. These behaviors, called rituals, are used because they lessen the anxiety created by the obsessions in OCD. Common rituals related to fears of contamination include excessive cleaning of objects (as in Alan's case), handwashing or showering, and repeated checking to be sure that an item is in its proper place, a door has been locked, the stove is turned off, or that some other situation or some person is safe. Other rituals involve arranging objects in very specific positions or orders, as Alan did; repeating actions such as taking clothes off and putting them on again; hoarding objects, through fear that something valuable will be lost; and counting repeatedly to a specific number.

The term compulsion, *as it applies to obsessive-compulsive disorder, refers to a recurrent urge to perform a specific behavior, such as scrubbing or washing, as a ritualized means of counteracting or preventing an obsessive concern or fear.*

The excessive handwashing, door checking, and other rituals seem to come from an uncertainty that the evidence supplied by the ordinary senses can be relied on—for exmple, seeing or feeling that the hands are clean or that the door is closed. Thus the person tries to overcome his or her doubt and achieve certainty by endlessly repeating the ritual.

Like Alan, some persons with OCD may behave compulsively without any obsessions. Rather than persistent thoughts of dirt or danger, they may simply feel compelled to perform a ritual and have difficulty explaining why, other than that they do not feel "right" unless they do it.

The essential distinction between the compulsions of OCD and "compulsive" eating, drinking, or gambling is that the latter behaviors are experienced as pleasurable and would not ordinarily be voluntarily stopped except for such consequences as obesity, a conviction for drunk driving, or the loss of money. By contrast, the compulsions of OCD are, as in Alan's case, experienced as unpleasant and undesirable, and can even cause tremendous anguish to those who have them. Indeed, the most recent, third edition of the American Psychiatric Association's *Diagnostic and Statistical Manual of Mental Disorders* (DSM III-R), which lists the standard criteria used to diagnose mental disorders, states that the obsessions of OCD must be "experienced, at least initially, as intrusive and senseless" and that the person affected by them must try to ignore, suppress, or neutralize them. The person affected by the obsessions must also be aware that they are products of his or her own mind and do not come from some "outside source." This last criterion differentiates OCD from disorders such as schizophrenia, in which the victim of a delusion (of being poisoned, for example) attributes it to a real, external source.

Who Has OCD?

A study done by the National Institute of Mental Health (NIMH), in which 18,000 Americans were interviewed in their homes, found that 1.3% had, within the previous month, experienced symptoms of OCD that were severe enough to meet the DSM III-R criteria. The study also found that as many as 3.3% of the interviewees had had the disorder at some time in the past. Another NIMH survey of 5,800 high school students in New Jersey found that 1% of them had OCD at the time of the study. The figures in these studies translate to approximately 5 million Americans who have OCD, including at least 1 million young people.

Other studies by the NIMH indicate that the disorder appears in specific patterns. Thus, half of all persons with OCD begin experiencing symptoms while they are children, in contrast to most people who develop psychiatric disorders. And among children, twice as many boys as girls develop the disorder. With increasing age, however, this ratio changes, so that among adults, equal numbers of women and men have OCD.

Varieties of OCD

The severity of OCD ranges from so mild as to not drive its victim into treatment to so severe that the victim spends the entire day doing nothing but performing rituals. As noted earlier, some people with OCD, like Alan, have compulsions but no obsessions, while others have obsessions but no compulsions, and some have both. Although it may occur in a single, brief episode, the malady, if not treated, usually lasts for life, with its severity alternately increasing and decreasing.

Similarly, OCD varies in the disruption it creates in the lives of its victims and their families. It may affect no one but the victim, or it may involve the entire family in extensive rituals performed in an attempt to reassure the victim and keep the peace in the house.

"Nobody Has To Suffer"

Two things about OCD are particularly important to remember. The first is that those who have it are not "crazy." According to Andrea Gitow, C.S.W., a research scientist in the Anxiety Disorders Clinic of the New York State Psychiatric Institute in New York City, the amazing thing about OCD is that it can be restricted to very specific situations and may not affect the entire personality. In the case of many OCD rituals and obsessions, explains Gitow, the victim can recognize their true nature and say, "This is senseless."

The second point to remember, however, is that even though persons with OCD know that their thoughts or behaviors are senseless, they cannot simply "stop" them. They doubt the messages from their own senses telling them that their hands are clean, the door is closed, or that they haven't hurt anyone, and no amount of reassurance from others can help them to stop.

The rest of this book will explore the history of obsessive-compulsive disorder, describe the theories about what causes it and the ways in which it manifests itself, and then focus on the two major types of treatment—drugs and behavioral therapy. Next it will explain how OCD can be differentiated from normal superstitions and childhood rituals, everyday obsessional or compulsive habits such as extreme neatness, and other psychiatric disorders such as phobias, depression, and schizophrenia. Finally, it will provide a list of sources from which OCD sufferers can get information and assistance.

CHAPTER 2

A HISTORICAL PERSPECTIVE

Obsessions and compulsions have been part of the human psyche for eons. The Egyptians, for example, used this amulet, representing an eye of the god Horus, to preserve and protect their health.

Although OCD was not defined until the 20th century, the behaviors to which it refers appear to have been known for centuries. Many examples of obsessive and compulsive symptoms have been recorded from as far back as the 15th century.

One very famous person who seems to have had the disorder was the great English writer and lexicographer Samuel Johnson (1709–84). Johnson's biographer James Boswell recorded many of his rituals and peculiar mannerisms that closely resemble those of OCD. Thus, says

The great English essayist and lexicographer Samuel Johnson exhibited behavior closely resembling that of OCD. Among his seeming rituals was the need to walk through doorways in a very precise manner—he insisted on exiting and reentering if his first effort to pass through a doorway erred in any way.

Boswell, Johnson had "an anxious care to go out or in at a door or passage by a certain number of steps from a certain point (so that) either his right or his left foot . . . should constantly make the first actual movement when he came close to the door or passage." And, continues Boswell, "When he had neglected or gone wrong in this sort of magical movement, I have seen him go back again" to do it right.

Persons with OCD also often manifest a need to condemn or undo their thoughts and actions by magical gestures. Johnson, when speaking, also seemed to have this characteristic. He "commonly held his head to one side towards his right shoulder," wrote Boswell, "and shook it in a tremulous manner, moving his body backwards and forwards, and rubbing his left knee in the same direction, with the palm of his hand." These actions, said another friend, "always appeared to me as if they were meant to reprobate some part of his past conduct."

Three centuries later, psychologist Robert O. Pasnau, in his book the *Diagnosis and Treatment of Anxiety Disorders*, described a 45-year-old businessman who had a similar ritual, with the compulsive need to end with his left foot on the last step when climbing a flight of stairs. Once, when late in boarding an airplane, the man ran up the stairway and ended with his right foot on the top step. He tried to take his seat but was so afraid the plane would crash that he jumped up, dashed out past the surprised stewardess, ran back down the stairs and came up again, this time ending on his left foot.

Judith Rapoport, M.D., a principal investigator of obsessive-compulsive disorder at the U.S. National Institute of Health in Bethesda, Maryland, and author of the book The Boy Who Couldn't Stop Washing.

In both religion and obsessive-compulsive disorder, ritualized behavior is used to ward off perceived dangers. This prayerful figurine was used in a religious ritual of the ancient Sumerian civilization of the Middle East.

OCD and Religion

According to Dr. Judith Rapoport, a principal investigator of obsessive-compulsive disorder at the U.S. National Institutes of Health, there are many connections between OCD and religion. For example, religions and people with OCD both make use of rituals and have concerns about purity of mind and body. In both religion and OCD, ritual is used to ward off some perceived danger. The difference is that in OCD, the ritual is taken to excess. In fact, so close was the connection between

The Protestant reformer Martin Luther suffered from obsessive blasphemous thoughts and from fears that he had omitted some act while performing mass for his parishioners.

religion and obsessive-compulsive behavior that in English the disorder was originally called "religious melancholy." The Roman Catholic church called it "scrupulosity," a term referring to unrealistic fears of having sinned. Moreover, a number of great religious figures seem to have had some version of OCD.

Thus, the Protestant reformer Martin Luther (1483–1546), who was a monk before becoming a leader of the Reformation in Germany, suffered from obsessive blasphemous thoughts, as well as from ideas that he had sinned by omitting some act while performing mass. These obsessions were so severe that he was driven to confess several times a day, at which point his superior had to discipline him.

Saint Ignatius Loyola (1491–1556), the founder of the Society of Jesus (the Jesuits), suffered from similar obsessions. In his *Spiritual Exercises*, a manual for devotion and prayer, Loyola described the obsessive thoughts and compulsions from which he suffered. He wrote that when he stepped inadvertently on two straws that happened to have the form of a cross, "there comes to me from 'without' a thought that I have sinned," while at the same time his mind told him that he had not really sinned. This conflict left him in a state of doubt.

Saint Ignatius Loyola, Spanish founder of the Society of Jesus, experienced various obsessive thoughts and exhibited compulsive behavior. Internal conflicts over whether inadvertent acts were in fact sinful often left him in a state of doubt.

English preacher and writer John Bunyan, author of Pilgrim's Progress, *described in his autobiography his experiences with both obsessive thoughts and compulsive behavior relating to his religious sincerity.*

Yet another religious obsessive was the English writer and preacher John Bunyan (1628–88), author of the famous allegory *Pilgrim's Progress*. In his autobiography, which he entitled *Grace Abounding to the Chief of Sinners*, Bunyan described the compulsive behavior evoked by an obsessive thought that he should sell Christ: "In labouring to gainsay and resist this wickedness, my . . . body . . . would be put

into action or motion . . . pushing or thrusting with my hands or elbows
. . . answering as fast as the destroyer said, *Sell him;* [by replying] *I
will not, I will not, I will not.*"

Yet Rapoport points out that these men, despite their obsessive
or compulsive behavior, were able to lead lives of tremendous ac-
complishment and influence. Nor can their malady be considered as
undercutting or invalidating their religious insights or the meaning of
their work.

In their *Malleus Maleficum* (Hammer of Witches)—a witch-
hunter's manual published in 1486—the German church writers Hein-
rich Kramer and James Sprenger, presented what to a modern physician
would look like a case of OCD as evidence of the state of being
"possessed by a devil." (Witches were thought to be possessed by Satan
or one of his demons.) The "possessed" person was a young man from
Bohemia. Whenever he "passed any church, and genuflected in honour
of the Glorious Virgin," wrote the two theologians, "the devil made

*In the 15th century,
witches were thought
to be possessed by
Satan or one of his evil
demons. A case of
such possession, which
today might well be
considered obsessive-
compulsive behavior,
was recorded in the
Malleus Maleficum, a
witch-hunters' manual
published in 1486.*

him thrust his tongue far out of his mouth." By identifying some cause for his behavior, their explanation no doubt provided some relief to the sufferer, who said he had no control over what he did. In contrast, many victims of OCD have no idea of the cause of their obsessions or compulsions and fear they must be "crazy."

Nineteenth-Century Attitudes

By the 19th century, science had progressed sufficiently so that it explained obsessive and compulsive behavior in terms of defects in intellectual or emotional functions rather than supernatural forces. In the first half of the century, French psychiatrists described such behavior as *folie du doute*—the "doubting madness"—in reference to the central problem in OCD of not being able to rely on one's senses to recognize (for example) that one's hands are really clean or that one hasn't hurt another person. In the second half of the century, English psychiatrists associated the terms "obsessive" and "compulsive" with this disorder.

A story in *Lavengro*, an 1851 autobiographical novel by the English writer George Borrow, exemplifies the 19th-century approach to OCD. In the story, a man who meets the narrator describes an experience he had as a boy, at a time when his mother was ill and he feared she would die. Early one morning as he lay in bed, the boy was visited by an impulse to climb a tall elm tree behind the house and "touch the topmost branch," and the feeling that if he did not, his mother would die. This was a very difficult feat, yet "the nervous feeling was within me," recounted the man, "impelling me upward." Having managed to touch the top of the tree by leaping from a high branch, he fell 20 feet down and was fortunately caught among the branches, which saved him from being killed.

When he returned, the boy found that his mother had taken a turn for the better and would recover. "Yet," said the storyteller, at the time he was performing this strange feat, he knew it to be absurd. "I was not weak enough," he explained, "to suppose that I had baffled . . . evil . . . by my daring feat. The psychologists of the time described obsessive-compulsive behavior in similar terms. It was this "impulse," "nervous feeling," or "mysterious dread" that they hoped to understand.

Freud's Theory

In 1909, Sigmund Freud published his famous "Notes upon a Case of Obsessional Neurosis," which presented a classic case of what Freud called "obsessional neurosis" and laid out a psychoanalytic theory of its causation.

The patient was a young man whose chief obsessions were fears that both his father and a young woman whom he loved would die. In fact, his father had already died several years earlier. The man's fears had begun when he was told a story about a punishment used in an Eastern country in which rats bored their way into a criminal's buttocks. The patient became obsessed with the idea that this was happening to the young woman and to his father and began a series of compulsive behaviors intended to stop it.

In addition to these obsessions, which led the man to consult Freud, he had many others. When younger, he had felt compelled to make up prayers that eventually took an hour and a half each day because, as with the Bohemian man, "something always inserted itself into his pious phrases and turned them into their opposite." He also felt he had to understand the exact meaning of everything that was said to him and would therefore ask people over and over, "What was it you just said?" yet was still left in a state of perpetual doubt.

Freud's analysis uncovered a number of symbolic meanings that rats had for the man, involving money, children, fear of infectious diseases (especially syphilis), and the penis. The story about the rat torture of criminals evoked repressed feelings from the man's childhood, especially in relation to his father and his feelings about his father's sexuality. Freud later theorized that such "obsessional neurosis" had its roots in early childhood and was caused by conflicts between unconscious, unacceptable aggressive and sexual impulses and a series of psychological defenses against the acting out of these impulses.

In his report of the case, Freud wrote that his analysis restored the man to mental health. However, because the patient was killed a few years later, in World War I, there is no way of knowing whether the cure was permanent or whether his symptoms would have recurred in later life, possibly during periods of stress.

Sigmund Freud (1856–1939), the Austrian physician and founder of psychoanalysis, whose "Notes upon a Case of Obsessional Neurosis" described a case of obsessive-compulsive disorder under the designation "obsessional neurosis" and provided a psychoanalytic theory of its causes.

Today, some practitioners of psychoanalytic therapy continue to see OCD as a disturbance of psychosexual development and treat it in a manner similar to that of Freud. However, according to Judith Rapoport and some other researchers who have worked extensively on OCD, psychoanalysis has not been helpful for most OCD patients. These experts point out that the psychoanalytic theory of OCD has been outdated by theories based on more recent discoveries indicating that OCD results from a biological abnormality in brain function. The newest and most effective treatments for OCD are based on this concept.

CHAPTER 3

WASHING, CHECKING, COUNTING, AND OTHER RITUALS

Fears of contamination by dirt and of infection by germs are two common obsessions in OCD. Both concerns extend well back into human history, as evidenced by this 17th-century illustration of methods for purging the body of unhealthy elements or "humors."

The obsessions and compulsions of OCD fall into several distinct categories. The most common obsessions involve fear of dirt and of contamination by germs, poisons, or body secretions; fear that something is wrong with the shape or functioning of a part of the body; fear of acting on persistent impulses to harm other people or oneself; constant worry that something has not been done properly (like locking a door); feelings that objects must be arranged in a particular place or order; forbidden sexual thoughts; blasphemous thoughts; and worry that something terrible will happen to a relative or friend.

As described in chapter 1, the rituals of OCD are usually responses to one or more obsessions. The most common rituals are excessive cleaning or washing to remove dirt or contamination; checking to be sure doors are closed, appliances are turned off, or nothing bad has happened; symmetrical ordering and arranging of objects; repeated counting to a certain number; repeating acts such as putting clothes on and taking them off, or writing and erasing words; and constantly seeking reassurance from family or friends that some feared event has not happened, or that some action (like locking the door) really has been performed.

Some compulsive behaviors are nonritualized. These include hoarding, such as collecting old newspapers and even saving garbage in response to a fear that something important might be thrown out. Some persons feel a compulsion to do everything extremely slowly.

Some examples will show how compulsions and obsessions work together.

Dirt and Contamination

In a study of 44 people with OCD, conducted by Drs. Steven A. Rasmussen and Ming T. Tsuang of the Department of Psychiatry at Brown University Medical School, the most common obsession was fear of contamination by dirt and infection by germs. Another prominent symptom was a "morbid (fear) of potentially cancer-causing chemicals such as insecticides or asbestos."

The ritual response to this type of obsession is generally cleaning or washing oneself, one's environment, or both. One nine-year-old boy told Judith Rapoport that when he was six years old, he had begun picking up things with his elbows because he thought he would get his hands dirty if he picked things up with his hands. By the time he was seven, he was washing his hands 35 times a day, said the boy.

Other children with OCD wash their hands as often as 150 times a day, or wash less often but keep washing for periods lasting up to several hours. Showering can also last for hours. Some people with the disorder scrub themselves to the point of damaging their skin and causing bleeding.

Others go to great lengths to avoid perceived contaminants. One 13-year-old boy not only had handwashing and showering rituals, but refused to go to school because "the school, the other children and the entire east side of (my) town were dirty." He used a paper towel to open doors and turn on faucets. Ultimately his fear of contamination made him unable to leave his house.

Some people with this type of fear cannot eat because they believe their food is contaminated. One woman's fear of contamination drove her to travel two hours on a train to buy soap because she believed all the bars of soap in her own city were contaminated.

The spread of AIDS has provided a new focus for persons whose OCD makes them afraid of contamination. According to Judith Rapoport, many OCD patients have developed obsessions and rituals that revolve around AIDS. They do this even though they are not in a high-risk group for AIDS and have no contact with anyone who is.

Besides fearing for themselves, people with OCD may fear that they have contaminated others. One nurse with the disorder had to leave her job at a hospital because of fear that she was contaminating syringes and intravenous needles. Later, the obsession spread to her home, where she began to doubt whether she was clean after using the toilet and developed washing rituals. She also had difficulty doing laundry because she feared she had put feces instead of soap in the washing machine.

Fears of Harm to Others

Fears that one has already hurt or will hurt another person were the second most common type of obsession in the study by Rasmussen and Tsuang. One woman in their study group was terrified that she would strangle her baby, and another woman felt that when in a store, she had to buy anything she touched because her touch had damaged it.

Similarly, John C. Nemiah, M.D., professor of psychiatry at the Dartmouth Medical School, describes a man who thought that his father would die every time he turned off a light. In order to prevent this from happening, he developed a ritual in which he would turn around, touch the switch, and say, "I take back that thought." Another man was afraid he would push someone off a subway platform as the train was coming in. Although he kept his arms pressed rigidly to his sides to prevent himself from doing this, he once became so obsessed with the possibility that he might already have pushed someone off despite his precautions that he had to call the transit authority to make sure that no such event had occurred.

Like this man, people who fear harm often engage in checking or reassurance rituals to assure themselves that they have not hurt someone they know or love, as well as engaging in avoidance rituals involving elaborate precautions against doing harm inadvertently. In one such case, a man who was afraid that he would inadvertently put poison in the coffeepot used by everyone at his job scrupulously avoided walking down the hallway where the pot was located. Afraid that he had harmed children playing in their yards whom he passed on his way home from work, he had his wife or children meet him at the bus stop to reassure him that the children were all right.

People with OCD may also fear that some agent other than themselves might do harm to another person. One 11-year-old girl had an intense fear that harm would come to her mother in a car accident, in an attack by a stranger, or from a bolt of lightning, among other sources. To relieve her terrible anxiety, the child used what scientists call *cognitive compulsions*. In this case, these compulsions involved saying an elaborate prayer, whose content varied according to what the child feared at the moment. If there was a storm outside, she might say: "Dear God, please don't let Mommy's car skid because of the rain. I'll be good if you don't let harm come to her." which she would say twice, then finish by saying "Our father who art in heaven, your faithful servant Lizzie."

Edvard Munch's painting The Dead Mother *represents the realization of one of the many manifestations of obsessive-compulsive disorder: an obsessive fear of danger or harm to a loved one. Such fears may lead to ritualized actions that are intended to prevent the occurrence of the feared event.*

The child felt compelled to repeat the entire prayer to herself three times. If she didn't say it perfectly all three times, she had to repeat the entire sequence, a procedure that could take up to 45 minutes. Once she completed it successfully, her anxiety dissipated, but she had to repeat the entire process whenever her mother was late coming home from work, or the weather was bad, or she heard a news report of a parent being murdered.

In addition to this, the child had a checking ritual in which she would call her mother as often as 12 times a day to be sure her mother was all right. She demanded to speak with her mother whether she was at a meeting, at lunch, or whatever. If she couldn't, she became paralyzed by distress and unable to engage in any other activity. The child also had an avoidance ritual about saying certain words. If, for example, someone said good-bye to her, she would insist that the person say another word as the last word before parting, thus magically undoing the effects of "good-bye."

Need for Symmetry and Order

The third most common obsession reported by Rasmussen and Tsuang was a need for symmetry and exactness. One of their patients, for example, had to walk exactly through the middle of a doorway and sit facing his therapist at an exact 90-degree angle. Patients with this type of obsession could not explain just why they had this need, except to express "a fear that something bad would happen if they did not 'even things up.'"

Alan, described in chapter 1, was an arranger. So was Peter, a 17-year-old Massachusetts boy who lived in a rigidly structured world that felt like a calendar. He had cleaning rituals that had to be performed at specific times. If he didn't finish the laundry by 3:00 P.M., for example, he felt that something dreadful would happen. Peter could not remember a time when he felt casual about the daily matters of life. Even as a small child in nursery school, he would be putting toys away in a box while the other children were playing, and at lunchtime he would fold napkins.

Other ordering rituals in OCD include taking steps of exactly the same length, retying one's shoelaces so the two loops of the bow are exactly the same length, and speaking with the same amount of stress on each syllable.

Counting and Repeating

Peter, the Massachusetts boy described above, had another ritual that involved reciting categories of words, such as boys' and girls' names, cities, and states. This had to begin with the letter *A* and be done in alphabetical order. He would go through all the categories of A's, then begin with the B's, and so on. Some other persons with OCD have rituals of repeating numbers or feel compelled to count up to a certain number between each performance of a specific action. Laura, a patient described by Judith Rapoport, had to count up to 50 between reading or writing every word in school (though not at home). Because this prevented her from reading aloud in class, she wound up in a school for the mentally handicapped even though there was nothing wrong with her intelligence.

A man described by John C. Nemiah developed a ritual that required him to tap his workbench on an electronics assembly line three times with his left hand, then three times with his right, then stamp on the floor three times with each foot in turn before he could solder two pieces of equipment together. At first this only slowed him down, but he then began to doubt whether he had really done the sequence correctly and had to repeat it. Soon the rituals took up his entire day and forced him to quit.

Sexual and Somatic Obsessions

Sexual obsessions generally involve fears that one will act on sexual urges that violate one's own principles or have a sexual identity of which one disapproves, such as homosexuality. A 16-year-old boy described by psychologist Fred Penzel, who works with persons affected by OCD, had many obsessions involving fears of committing suicide, being schizophrenic, and being homosexual. His ritual response to these thoughts was to compulsively ask people close to him whether they thought he was gay, as well as asking them about his other obsessions in order to be reassured that these things were not so.

Somatic obsessions are worries about one's body that may provoke the need for constant checking to assure oneself of being physically all right. Rasmussen and Tsuang describe the case of a surgeon whose obsession of making sure that he did not have a hernia in his groin drove him to examine himself so often that he wound up creating an open sore. Another case of somatic obsessions involved a woman who examined her breasts as often as 100 times a day to make sure she did not have cancer.

While teenagers are normally intensely concerned with their appearance, those with OCD go much further than the norm. Jessica, a 16-year-old Massachusetts girl, had many rituals related to her appearance. Her hairdo and makeup had to be precisely correct. She spent at least an hour in front of the mirror before she could go to school, literally combing her hair one hair at a time, then spraying it to fix it in place. If she found a spot of any size on her clothes, she became extremely upset and had to run upstairs and plow through her closet, trying on a dozen different outfits to find something that was acceptable

Obsessions with the appearance and function of one's body—known as somatic obsessions—and with one's sexual identity, behavior, and relationships are other ideas that trouble the minds of some persons with OCD.

to wear. The laces of her sneakers had to be tied in a precise manner, using an intricate braiding technique she had developed.

Nonritualized Compulsions

As noted earlier, some compulsive behaviors do not appear as rituals. One woman with a compulsion to hoard said that she did so because of a fear that she "might lose something important." As time passed, she required more and more vigilant checking to be sure she had not lost anything. Originally worrying about truly valuable items such as jewelry, she soon began to worry about throwing anything out for fear she might discard something important. Eventually she could not throw out anything, and her house "was . . . overflowing with junk and garbage."

Another nonritualized compulsive behavior is slowness. The rituals of OCD can themselves take up so much time that they prevent their victim from leading a normal life. But in some persons, slowness is the predominant symptom of OCD. These people feel they must do everything extremely slowly to make sure they do it properly and therefore require hours each day to get dressed, washed, and out of the house. Slowness and hoarding are less common than other forms of OCD, but can severely incapacitate those afflicted with them.

Combining Different Rituals and Obsessions

Someone afflicted with OCD may have several types of obsessions and rituals or may develop new ones as time passes, while others fall away. A six-year-old boy described by Judith Rapoport and NIMH pediatrician Dr. Susan Swedo became obsessed with tornadoes after seeing a television documentary about them and watching the movie *The Wizard of Oz*. In response to his fear he developed checking rituals, such as looking out the window to see if the sky was clear. In an attempt to control his anxiety about the possibility of a tornado, he learned a great deal about meteorology.

The child's obsession then shifted to a concern with power lines and electrocution, which involved new checking rituals. He checked light switches and outlets in his home and rode his bike along the path of a nearby high-tension power line to "check that the posts were strong enough." Meanwhile, he also had more general fears that he and his family would be harmed and therefore devised other rituals to protect them.

When he reached puberty, his obsession became one of fear of harm to himself from chemicals or germs. He began compulsive handwashing and drank large amounts of water "to flush out the poisons from his body." He also checked his house for chemicals and vacuumed it every day. Finally, he became afraid he might accidentally kill himself.

Puzzling Aspects of Rituals

It is hard to understand exacly how the rituals in OCD function to make its victims feel better. Why some people have rituals without obsessions is also puzzling.

Researcher Andrea Gitow remarks that "the most baffling thing about OCD is the sensation in almost every patient of something feeling 'right' or 'not right.'" The patients themselves cannot explain exactly what this is, she observes.

She also notes that the sensation that tells a patient when a ritual can be stopped because it has been performed enough varies among different patients and even in the same patient. The degree of repetition that is "right" on one day may not be enough on the next.

Moreover, the symptoms of OCD are the same in very different cultures, says Judith Rapoport. She cites studies in China, England, Sweden, India, and the Sudan showing that people with OCD in these different countries have the same kinds of fears and rituals, and that the behavior most often seen among them is washing. This, says Rapoport, suggests that these behaviors are not based on specific elements of a nation's culture and psychology but derive instead from a deeper level of biologically fixed, innate behavior patterns that are somehow expressed in people with the disorder. Chapter 5 will discuss this biological basis, but first, it will be helpful to discuss the origins of OCD and some of the ways in which it affects those in whom it develops.

CHAPTER 4

THEY CAN'T "JUST STOP"

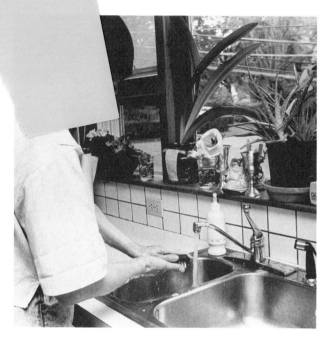

Repeated handwashing and other forms of compulsive behavior may consume hours per day in the lives of persons with OCD, interfering with their social and vocational functioning.

Despite her OCD and the distress it caused, Lizzie, the 11-year-old girl described in chapter 3, was a very social child with many friends and had a "lovely, charming personality," observes her therapist, Andrea Gitow. "Apart from her OCD," explains Gitow, "Lizzie was also a completely well-adjusted, intelligent 11-year-old who did well at school."

Indeed, most people with OCD are otherwise normal and can lead functional lives that include work, family, and socializing, and young people with the disorder seem to have intelligence in the high normal range, according to psychological studies done in primary and secondary schools. For their part, adults with OCD are often extremely successful, including many businessmen, doctors, lawyers, and other professionals.

Despite this, obsessive-compulsive behavior can create unhappiness in the personal and social lives of its victims, as in the case of Alan and many of the other persons described in this book. Because persons affected with OCD often function so well, other people are likely to assume that their obsessions and compulsions are under control. This may lead to considerable misunderstanding and conflict. Apart from creating great difficulties in family life, OCD may prevent its victims from marrying and even creating intimate relationships at any level.

How Does It Start?

OCD appears in different ways. In some it begins suddenly, explains Dr. Fred Penzel; for others it creeps up gradually. "Only when they're truly dysfunctional do others realize it's getting out of hand."

About one-fourth of Rasmussen and Tsuang's patients described a specific event that seemed to trigger the onset of their OCD. These were usually stressful events such as the birth of a child, a job promotion, or the death of a family member. Nevertheless, says Andrea Gitow, "We find there's usually not a triggering or traumatic event." Furthermore, even when such an event occurs it cannot be thought of as causing the disorder, but only as a stressful situation that worsened an already existing predisposition to OCD in a particular person.

For Sam, the 16-year-old boy described in chapter 3, who feared that he would commit suicide or was schizophrenic or homosexual, the triggering event of his OCD had been a suicide attempt by a girl in his school when he was 14. Following this, he became obsessed with the idea of suicide, and his obsessions then spread to his appearance, his performance as an athlete, and the idea that he might be homosexual.

In another case, OCD was set off in a teenage boy who read in a newspaper about a piece of molding that fell from a building and hit a passerby. He became obsessed about this and could not walk down the street without constantly looking up at buildings to be sure this wouldn't happen to him. In time his preoccupation spread to other kinds of danger.

Varieties of OCD

Besides beginning in different ways, OCD can cause its victims different degrees of emotional distress and functional impairment. Rasmussen and Tsuang observed that the OCD in their 44 patients was episodic, continuous, or deteriorative. As its name suggests, episodic OCD takes the form of recurring episodes of illness, each lasting for only a limited period. Although obsessive-compulsive symptoms may remain after an episode, the victim can usually integrate these into his or her life in such a way as to be able to function in a completely normal manner.

Continuous OCD is marked not only by severe episodes of the disorder during stressful periods but also by symptoms between these episodes that impair the victims' social and vocational lives, although they can still function at home and on the job.

The symptoms of persons with deteriorative OCD—a progressively worsening illness—can become so severe that they completely incapacitate their victims socially or occupationally. These people may have few or no periods during which their ability to function improves and may spend all their waking hours compulsively doing rituals.

According to Rasmussen and Tsuang, the overwhelming majority of the patients in their study followed a "chronic waxing and waning course," with stress-related exacerbations and mild to moderate symptoms between overt episodes of OCD. John H. Greist, M.D., of the Obsessive-Compulsive Information Center at the University of Wisconsin, agrees that most cases of OCD follow this type of fluctuating course. If the disorder is not treated, it will generally last for the rest of its victim's life, although its specific symptoms are likely to change. Thus, someone with OCD might during one episode be obsessed with fears of harming others, and therefore perform checking rituals, and during the next episode exhibit a fear of contamination expressed through washing rituals.

Hiding OCD

Because they have developed such ingenious ways to hide their rituals, explains Judith Rapoport, persons with OCD "are the world's greatest actors and actresses." Researchers Rasmussen and Tsuang found that many of their patients were able to hide symptoms that produced "significant social or occupational impairment" from their wives, husbands, and other family members. Thus, children who feel humiliated and ashamed of their rituals may disguise handwashing, for example, as needing to go to the bathroom frequently. One teenage girl, identified by the high school survey described in chapter 1, told Judith

In order to hide repeated hair brushing and other forms of compulsive behavior from their peers, young persons with obsessive-compulsive disorder may devise complicated explanations to cover the repeated periods of absence in which they engage in such behavior.

Rapoport that her disguise for her checking or washing rituals was to cultivate the impression that she was scatterbrained and always "running to the bathroom" to "do her hair." According to Rapoport, children say that controlling their rituals in public takes huge amounts of energy and that when they are home they simply must "let go" and perform them.

Effects on Social Life and Relationships

Although most people with OCD remain able to work, the disorder has severe effects on various aspects of their lives. Several studies that followed adults with OCD over a period of years found that many experienced social isolation and either had no sexual relationships at all or, if married, had marital problems.

A long-term study of youngsters with OCD at the University of California Neuropsychiatric Institute found that all of them had problems with friends and social life after as many as 14 years and that none of them were married. The most positive experiences reported by members of the group were the ability to attend college and to find jobs in which being compulsive was an advantage or at least socially acceptable.

In another study, of 25 children who were interviewed at the NIMH, Martine F. Flament, M.D., and her colleagues found that from two to seven years later, over half of the youngsters still had moderate or severe anxiety, depression, or both, and that six of the group had attempted suicide.

Not surprisingly, nearly all people with OCD are depressed, says Dr. Harvey Clarizio, professor of psychology at Michigan State University. "The long hours spent in repetitive thoughts and actions seem to take the pleasure out of once enjoyable activities such as sports, reading, and sex. The constant preoccupation with ruminations and compulsions leaves little time or energy for friends, family, or school."

Children and adolescents who spend their time ritualizing instead of socializing don't develop the social skills they need to create successful friendships and love relationships, says Andrea Gitow. This seems to be one reason why people with OCD are less likely to get married, she explains. Another reason would be an inability to give up their rituals in order to make the kind of compromises needed to live with another person.

Problems at School

Even if they successfully hide their OCD, children and teenagers may still find that it interferes with schoolwork. Its effects can include slowness caused by the attempt to write perfectly, making it difficult for the student to finish tests and submit papers on time; trouble with note taking from attempts to write down every word a teacher speaks; and frequent absences, to avoid ridicule and teasing by schoolmates.

Jessica, the 16-year-old described in chapter 4, had no problems in the classroom despite the rituals she performed in connection with her

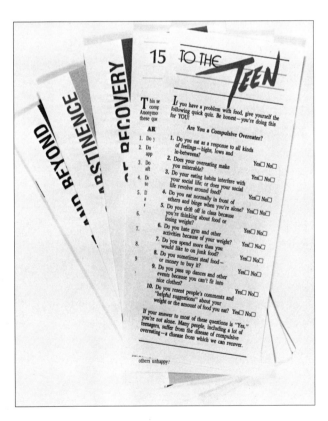

Most often beginning in childhood, and occasionally developing in adolescence, obsessive-compulsive behavior presents a great many problems for the young people it affects, interfering with social life, schoolwork, vocational development, and many other aspects of maturation.

appearance. Yet she also had homework rituals that kept her up until midnight, pushing her to read, underline, write, and rewrite repeatedly until her work was absolutely perfect.

Family Problems

The lack of support and even outright criticism to which they are subject is a source of stress, anxiety, and depression for people with OCD. Much of this begins with parents who do not understand why their children cannot "just stop that odd behavior." Further stress comes from well-intentioned relatives outside the immediate family who cannot understand the kinds of problems OCD creates and are critical of how the family handles them.

As a result, says social worker Barbara Livingston and Dr. Rasmussen in their booklet *Obsessive-Compulsive Disorder in Children and Adolescents*, the family "usually feel[s] distraught, bewildered, overwhelmed, and frustrated."

One problem for families is that people with OCD are likely to involve other family members in their obsessions and rituals. This is particularly true in the case of fears of contamination, with the OCD victim often worrying about contamination that other family members might bring into the house. A common request, says Dr. John Greist, is that family members have separate shoes for "inside" and "outside" wear; further demands are that they have "inside" and "outside" clothing, take showers after returning home, and not let any outsiders into the home. At first the family may go along with this to avoid the anxiety and arguments of the affected family member. Later, however, they may become caught up in a web of burdensome restrictions that still do not allay the victim's anxiety.

Families may also be drawn into checking rituals. Marge Lenane, M.S.W., of the Child Psychiatry Branch of the NIMH, describes a case in which an OCD patient's mother helped check the house to make sure that all was safe but then would have to get up in the middle of the night to do it again.

The extent to which families may try to accommodate an OCD victim's compulsion is demonstrated by the case of a woman whose compulsive need for symmetry drove her to line up all of the food containers in her refrigerator in a particular pattern and to measure the distances between them. So exacting was her condition that she kept a ruler next to the refrigerator and demanded that when her husband took out the milk container, he take a measurement upon returning it, to be certain that he had put it back precisely in its proper place. To satisfy her, he complied.

In addition to participating in the victim's rituals to keep the peace, families also choose not to let the victim perform any rituals or may refuse to acknowledge or allow any compulsions to be expressed in

A mother's or father's belief of having somehow "given" OCD to a son or daughter may produce considerable guilt in that parent. Conversely, parents who have themselves had the disorder may be overly tolerant of its existence in their children.

their presence. No matter which response is chosen, say some experts, it may evoke powerful feelings and frustrations for all family members.

In many cases involving children with OCD, one of the parents also has the disorder, since it tends to run in families, as discussed in chapter 5.

Parents with OCD may feel guilt for having "given" their condition to a son or daughter or may be unable to admit to the child that they themselves have the disorder. The parent may also want to be different from a parent of his or her own who was intolerant of the condition and may therefore be too indulgent with a son or daughter afflicted with OCD. If there is conflict between the parents, one may use the fact that the other "passed on" OCD to the child as a weapon against the other.

OCD is also hard on the siblings of children who have it. These other children often feel neglected and unloved because of time and attention given to the child with the condition. Not only may siblings feel jealous, but they may feel the need to take on extra responsibility. In one family, an older brother had to time his 14-year-old sister's two-hour shower to reassure her that she had washed enough.

Siblings may also suffer teasing from their own friends and from classmates when a brother or sister with OCD goes to the same school, making things worse all around.

Self-Treatment

In a desperate attempt to control their anxiety, some persons with OCD turn to alcohol or other drugs. Pointing out that embarrassment over their symptoms may inhibit their ability to seek treatment, "they try to cope on their own," says psychologist Fred Penzel. But while drinking calms them, dampening the urge to perform their rituals, says Penzel, they may also develop an association between feelings of relief and the act of drinking, making them more likely to drink the next time their symptoms occur.

According to Martine F. Flament, and a group of colleagues at the NIMH, more constructive ways of coping with OCD involve keeping busy, especially with activities governed by an external schedule. Exercise, they say, is also helpful. They also report that some of the youngsters in their study groups have developed a "trick" of getting others to "take the responsibility" for their actions, which has helped them to stop ritualizing enough to lock a door once and leave it behind without having to go back repeatedly to see that it is locked.

According to Dr. Flament and her colleagues, some of the young patients at the NIMH even invented their own self-treatment program, exposing themselves with tremendous determination to a stimulus such as dirt that triggered their need to perform rituals, and then forcing themselves to endure this without performing the rituals. This resembles the behavioral therapy that is now a major form of treatment for OCD, as will be discussed in chapter 7. Before going into this, however, it will help to explore some of the factors known to cause OCD.

CHAPTER 5

WHAT CAUSES OCD?

One of the effects of OCD may be the compulsive, ritualized need to stop and count or repeat a series of letters or words between parts of a school lesson or other exercise or activity. This can slow the learning of new material or stop it entirely, thus interfering greatly with academic performance.

Laura, whose need to count to 50 between each word she read or wrote was described in chapter 3, had had OCD from the age of seven. Laura had no idea why she felt compelled to perform this counting ritual. Remembering a science fiction movie she had seen, she decided when she was eight that her ritual was a way in which Martians were using her to make contact with Earth.

According to Judith Rapoport, a number of other patients whose OCD began during early childhood also "entertained a science fiction

Many persons whose obsessive-compulsive disorder began during childhood have described the feeling of having been controlled by forces or agents from outer space, calling this the only explanation they could find for their troubling thoughts and behaviors.

hypothesis about being controlled from outer space because it was the only remotely understandable model they could find."

This notion is not very different from the medieval theory of rituals and obsessions resulting from being possessed by the devil, as described in chapter 2. Both concepts assume that the person enacting the rituals is being controlled by an external force. The development of modern psychology, however, has shifted the quest for the cause of the rituals from external sources to factors inside the OCD victim.

Psychoanalytic Theory

As noted in chapter 2, psychoanalytic theorists, following Freud, saw the symptoms of OCD as symbolizing unconscious conflicts over

‑sonally unacceptable sexual and aggressive impulses. ‑ theory maintains that the symptoms of OCD serve to ‑xiety that stems from these impulses. The widespread ‑out dirt and fears of harming others led psychoanalysts ‑ the disorder has its origins in what is known as the ‑ase of a child's early development. In this phase of ‑ich occurs from about eight months to two years of ‑ent and urination are thought to produce pleasure, ‑ imposed discipline of toilet training is thought to ‑mpulses at the same time.

‑ychoanalytic therapy based on this theory has ‑ful in helping persons who have OCD. Although ‑y psychiatrists and psychologists still try to treat victims of OCD by seeking the unconscious feelings or thoughts that might lie beneath their symptoms, experts generally agree that in most cases, and certainly in the most severe ones, psychoanalytic therapy does not eliminate the obsessions and compulsions of OCD.

Following Sigmund Freud, many early psychoanalytic theorists believed that the symptoms of OCD reflected unconscious conflicts within the mind of the affected individual, having to do with impulses toward actions that were socially or personally unacceptable.

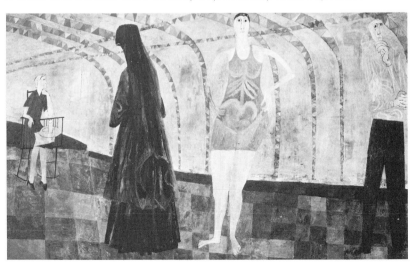

Learning Theory

There is some evidence that persons raised in religions that have many ritualistic practices may be more susceptible to developing OCD. Researchers Steven Rasmussen and Ming Tsuang found that many of their OCD patients had had an extremely strict religious upbringing whose components became part of their obsessions or rituals. This association between religious ritual and the development of OCD suggests that some aspects of OCD have to do with a person's childhood learning experiences.

Although the newest theories, developed during the 1980s, suggest that the cause of OCD is largely biological, involving abnormalities in the biochemistry of the brain, the field of psychology known as *learning theory* has, like psychoanalysis, focused on a psychological cause for OCD. Learning theory deals with how knowledge is acquired and modified as new learning occurs. It maintains that anxiety is a learned response to particular stimuli. For someone in whom OCD develops, an open door, the possibility that one's mother has been in an accident, and other specific thoughts and objects become associated with anxiety. The person then performs (or may discover by

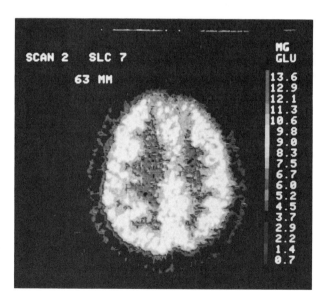

The technique known as positron emission tomography, or PET, has provided evidence for an abnormality within the brain structures known as the basal ganglia in obsessive-compulsive disorder. The illustration shows a PET scan of the brain made from above.

accident) an act—such as checking the door or saying a prayer—that is intended to relieve each specific anxiety. If these acts successfully relieve the anxiety, they are more likely to be performed again and thus become reinforced. Gradually, these acts become firmly established as compulsions.

Although learning theory leaves many questions about OCD unanswered (such as why dirt and aggression are the most frequent sources of obsessions and compulsions), it does provide an explanation of how rituals are acquired and maintained. More important, it offers a principle according to which OCD can be treated. This focuses on breaking the connection between the original stimulus, such as dirt, and the anxiety it provokes (as discussed in greater detail in chapter 7).

Biochemical Abnormalities

The most recent theories about the origin of OCD are based on the effectiveness of certain drugs in decreasing its symptoms. In the 1970s it was discovered that *clomipramine*, a drug used to treat depression, could reduce the symptoms of most OCD victims who took it. If a drug, which is a chemical substance that affects the functioning of the brain, can relieve the effects of a disorder, it follows that the disorder must come from something askew in the brain's chemistry in the first place. The beneficial effect of clomipramine suggested that at least one of the factors causing OCD is a biological abnormality in the brain.

Research along several different lines has supported such a biological basis for OCD. Clomipramine, as well as other drugs subsequently discovered to be effective against OCD, acts on a specific chemical substance in the brain, known as serotonin. Serotonin belongs to the family of natural chemical substances called neurotransmitters—substances released from nerve cells (neurons) in the brain that carry messages from these neurons to other neurons.

The neurons and neurotransmitters that are found within the brain are highly specialized and belong to distinct systems that perform highly specialized functions. Serotonin appears to transmit messages

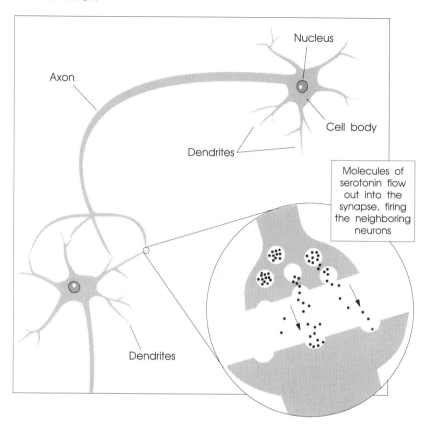

Serotonin is a substance that carries messages between nerve cells in specific structures within the brain. A deficiency of serotonin in several of these brain structures has been suggested as the biological basis of obsessive-compulsive disorder.

that inhibit impulsiveness, aggression, anxiety, and suicidal tendencies. Accordingly, it seems very possible that an incorrect amount of serotonin in certain parts of the brain might be a factor in causing the behaviors that constitute the symptoms of OCD.

Scientists have also found that neurons that release serotonin occur plentifully in certain brain structures that regulate these kinds of behaviors. Among these structures are the orbital gyri, located just over the eyes, which regulate the appropriateness of social behavior, and the basal ganglia, which lie deep within the brain and relay messages between the front part of the brain and the lower motor and sensory areas. Some experts believe that an increase in the *metabolism*, or degree of physical and chemical activity in the orbital gyri, combined with an inability of the lower structures to properly handle the greater number of messages produced by the gyri, may lie behind the excessive behaviors of OCD.

Further evidence for the involvement of the basal ganglia in OCD comes from studies done with a new brain-imaging technique known as *positron emission tomography*, or PET. In this technique, a patient is given glucose, a chemical that is normally metabolized by the brain but that in this case carries a "tag" or "label" consisting of a radioactive isotope. A gamma-ray detector picks up the radiation emitted by the labeled glucose, producing an image of how the brain metabolizes glucose. PET scans of persons with OCD show an abnormally high rate of glucose metabolism in the structure known as the caudate nucleus, which is a part of the basal ganglia.

Thus an abnormality in brain function, probably consisting of a deficiency of serotonin (although scientists are not yet certain of this), seems to be a major component of OCD. It is also possible that other neurotransmitter systems are involved in the disorder. Even this knowledge, however, reveals little about the ultimate causes or triggers of OCD or about effective treatment for the condition. The abnormalities involving serotonin may even result from, rather than be the cause of, OCD.

Genetic Theories

In addition to the findings in PET scans, another line of evidence suggests that the biochemical abnormalities implicated in OCD may be inherited. According to Harvey Clarizio, at least 20% of persons who have OCD have a near relative who also has the disorder. This makes the disorder more prevalent among these families than among the population at large.

According to Dr. John Greist, four or more consecutive generations of some families have had OCD. It is true that in some cases transmission of the disorder may not be genetic, since children can also learn the behaviors of OCD from their parents. However, the specific obses-

Research scientists discussing the significance of chromosomes. Chromosomes contain genes, which carry information determining an individual's biological makeup. A number of therapists and research scientists have noted the occurrence of OCD in more than one generation of a particular family. This has led to the suggestion that a susceptibility to the disorder may be passed along from parents to children through the genes.

sions and compulsions of the family members observed by Greist differ from one generation to the next, suggesting that what was transmitted was not a learned behavior but the tendency to react to stress with obsessions or compulsions, or both.

Similarly, a few studies of twins have suggested an inherited genetic basis for OCD, although the mechanism of the inheritance is again unknown.

Related Neurological Disorders

Still another line of evidence for OCD having a biochemical origin is its tendency to be associated within the same patients with other neurological disorders that also involve dysfunction of the basal ganglia. One of these disorders is *Tourette's syndrome*, which produces bouts of uncontrollable tics (muscle movements and sounds) in the person it affects. According to Judith Rapoport, about one-third of all persons who have Tourette's syndrome also have obsessions and compulsions like those of OCD, and conversely, many people with OCD have facial twitches, jerky movements of their hands or feet, and other tics. Moreover, Tourette's syndrome tends to run in the same families that have members afflicted with OCD.

Among other neurological disorders that affect the basal ganglia and are associated with the symptoms of OCD is epilepsy. Another such disorder is a form of encephalitis (a viral infection of the brain) that leaves its victims with involuntary twitches and movements after they recover. A third such condition is *Sydenham's chorea*, a brain disease characterized by involuntary, rapid, jerky movements affecting the ability to speak as well as the arms and legs. As many as a third of the victims of Sydenham's chorea also have OCD.

Related Compulsive Disorders

According to psychiatrist Dr. Carol N. Pleasants of the Pioneer Clinic in St. Paul, Minnesota, the disorder known as *trichotillomania*, or "hair-pulling compulsion," has many similarities to OCD. It frequently begins around the age of 12 or 13, and its onset is often associated with a stressful event. Furthermore, many people who have trichotillomania also have symptoms of OCD, and the conditions tend to run in the same families. People who have this disorder feel a compulsion to pull their hair out. This compulsion may involve any part of the body where hair grows, including the head, face, chest, legs, or pubic area. The victims of trichotillomania often experience anxiety that is relieved by the hair pulling and may engage in this for minutes or even hours a day. Many play with the hair or dispose of it in some ritualistic manner after pulling it out, such as by touching it to their lips or eating it.

The inability of people with trichotillomania to prevent themselves from pulling their hair and their need to disguise the resulting bald spots with wigs, eyebrow pencil, and false eyelashes causes shame and feelings of low self-worth and often expose the victim to ridicule from family or friends.

The similarities between trichotillomania and OCD are such that experts are beginning to view trichotillomania as a subtype of OCD. However, it may be related to OCD in a manner more like that of Tourette's syndrome, which involves a dysfunction of the same brain areas as OCD but is treated with medications that affect a different neurotransmitter system. Although the same treatments—drugs and behavioral therapy—that are effective for OCD also work for trichotil-lomania, the latter disorder differs from OCD in that almost all of the persons in whom it develops are female. The NIMH now estimates that between 4 and 8 million people have trichotillomania and that about 90% of them are female. Another difference is that trichotillomania does not involve obsessive thoughts.

The OCD constellation of disorders also includes compulsive nail-biting, or onychophagia, as well as trichotillomania, notes Fred Penzel. These disorders and OCD, and even Tourette's syndrome, he explains, may turn out to be different expressions of the same gene.

Environmental Factors

All of the data so far gathered suggest that an individual must have some biochemical predisposition—perhaps an inherited one—in order to develop OCD. What determines whether someone actually *does* develop OCD, however, are environmental factors such as family experiences and the amount of stress on someone who is predisposed to the disorder, say many experts. "It seems probable that there is an interaction between a genetic predisposition, biochemical factors, and experiences in life that either encourage or protect against the development of OCD," explains John Greist.

These environmental factors, say Barbara Livingston and Steven Rasmussen in the pamphlet *Learning to Live with OCD*, include mother-infant interaction, family functioning, and overall stress. In particular, young people subject to high levels of stress may respond by developing symptoms of OCD.

Although it appears likely that some people have a hereditary or other biologic predisposition toward obsessive-compulsive disorder, environmental factors seem to play the final role in determining whether or not the disorder actually develops.

One example of this last situation was described by Shelley Messing, C.S.W., a therapist who specializes in treating survivors of child abuse. The case involved a woman who as a young girl had lived with an alcoholic, violent father and a violent older brother. In response to this, she had developed rituals that helped her to feel less afraid. Thus, she believed that if she put pennies in all the cracks in the sidewalk or folded her hands in particular patterns and sat on her feet in bed in certain positions, her parents would stop fighting.

When Rosemary was 12, her father left the family. She soon felt safer, and her rituals stopped, although other disorders, including drug abuse and anorexia, took their place. Her OCD had been a way of coping with severe anxiety and distress.

Calling the compulsive behavior of children who grow up in abusive families "adaptive," Messing says that it gives them a sense of control over their lives, the belief that if they perform their rituals they can survive.

Yet many people who develop OCD have not experienced abuse or other mistreatment. The stressful event that triggers the disorder can even be a happy one. This supports the view of many investigators that a genetic predisposition is the strongest factor in determining who develops OCD.

CHAPTER 6

DRUG TREATMENT

Three medications have proven effective in alleviating obsessive-compulsive disorder. All three belong to the class of drugs known as antidepressants, *because their major use is in treating depression. Only one of them—clomipramine—has been approved in the United States for treating obsessive-compulsive disorder.*

In the past, psychoanalysis was the only form of treatment available to persons with OCD and, as noted earlier, is not particularly effective. Since the early 1970s, however, two new, effective forms of treatment have been developed: drug treatment and behavior therapy. This chapter will discuss drug treatment for OCD, and chapter 7 will describe how behavior therapy is used to treat the disorder.

Anti-Obsessive Drugs

The medications that are effective against OCD come from a group of drugs called antidepressants. Although all these drugs were originally developed to relieve depression, three of them have been found effective against the symptoms of OCD as well. These three anti-obsessive drugs are clomipramine, which was briefly discussed in chapter 5, fluoxetine, and fluvoxamine, which is not available in the United States.

All three drugs enhance the effect of serotonin in transmitting messages between nerve cells. They do this by slowing the rate at

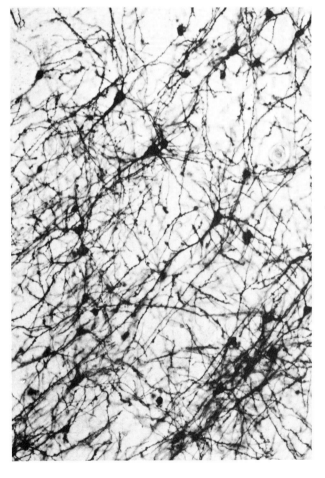

A microphotograph of neurons in the human brain, magnified 100 times.

which the same neurons that produce and release serotonin reabsorb this neurotransmitter (which is what these neurons usually do). As a result, more serotonin remains in the tiny gap, or synapse, that separates neighboring nerve cells, and therefore more of the substance is free to carry messages. For this reason the family of medications to which clomipramine, fluoxetine, and fluvoxamine belong are called *serotonin reuptake inhibitors*.

Although the efficacy of these medications in treating OCD suggests that the disorder is caused by a serotonin deficiency, as discussed in chapter 5, the chemistry of the brain is very complex, and this idea may well be simplistic. Judith Rapoport, for example, suggests that the anti-obsessive drugs may actually work by affecting other brain chemicals that are themselves affected by serotonin levels.

The complexity of this issue was demonstrated by Dr. Michael A. Jenike and his colleagues at the Massachusetts General Hospital. They found that sertraline, a drug that worked very specifically on the serotonin system, was also the least effective of several such drugs in reducing OCD symptoms. As a result, Jenike and his group suggested that drugs acting on other neurotransmitters in addition to serotonin might be more effective for treating OCD.

Dr. Christopher J. McDougle of Yale University and several colleagues presented evidence that at least one other neurotransmitter system may be involved in OCD. They found that a 45-year-old man with OCD experienced a severe increase in handwashing and arranging rituals, as well as in a left shoulder jerk that he had had for years, after taking cocaine. Because cocaine enhances the activity of the neurotransmitter known as *dopamine*, McDougle and his colleagues suggested that systems of neurons that use dopamine to transmit their messages might also be a factor in causing OCD symptoms.

Clomipramine

Clomipramine is currently the only drug approved in the United States for treating OCD. Many studies have shown that it reduces and even eliminates obsessions and compulsions. It is usually taken in the form

Although clomipramine has proven effective in many cases of OCD and is available in the United States by prescription, it is important to recognize that drug treatment for the disorder does not cure it. By easing the symptoms of the disorder, however, drug therapy may permit the concurrent use of other treatment methods such as behavior therapy.

of pills two or three times a day. The dose is then usually increased gradually over a period of several weeks until the drug produces a response. Later, the dose may be reduced to the smallest amount needed to minimize the patient's symptoms.

Like other antidepressants, clomipramine causes side effects. The most common of these is a dry mouth. Clomipramine's other side

effects include constipation, sweating, and nausea, as well as insomnia and overexcitement. The most dangerous aspect of clomipramine is that an overdose can cause a seizure.

In addition to producing side effects, for some people clomipramine is simply ineffective. Other anti-obsessive drugs can be prescribed for these patients.

Fluoxetine

Like clomipramine, fluoxetine is a serotonin reuptake inhibitor that is approved in the United States for treating depression. It has also shown effectiveness in treating OCD, but unlike clomipramine it has not been approved for this use. Although fluoxetine has not been studied as completely as clomipramine in connection with OCD, it is currently being evaluated in the treatment of persons for whom clomipramine is ineffective against OCD or for whom it creates intolerable side effects.

Studies at the Anxiety Disorders Clinic of the New York State Psychiatric Institute have suggested that in children and adolescents, fluoxetine has less severe side effects than clomipramine, says Andrea Gitow, one of the researchers in these studies. Fluoxetine may cause jitteriness, overexcitement, and insomnia, but it seems less likely than clomipramine to cause a number of other unpleasant side effects and is less harmful in the case of an overdose.

Fluvoxamine

Fluvoxamine, available as an antidepressant in most European countries, is still an experimental drug in the United States and not approved for any use by the U. S. Food and Drug Administration. It is therefore not readily available for investigation as a treatment for OCD, although some patients with the disorder are receiving it in experimental programs. Its most frequent side effects are nausea, headache, and overexcitement.

Effectiveness of Anti-Obsessive Drugs

According to Judith Rapoport, it is impossible to predict which patients with OCD will benefit from anti-obsessive drugs. Dr. John Greist reports that from 50% to 80% of patients who use these drugs show improvement, but Fred Penzel points out that for drug treatment to be effective against OCD, it is important for the patient to find a psychiatrist who is knowledgeable about the disorder. Many psychiatrists have too little experience with OCD to prescribe medication for it appropriately, he explains, and adds that OCD is also more difficult to treat with drugs than are other psychological disorders, since some patients respond to one drug and not another.

It is also important to remember that drug treatment for OCD is not a cure; it simply controls the symptoms so that people can get on with their lives. This means that in most cases, when people stop taking the medications, their symptoms return. Often, however, the dose of a drug can be reduced after some time has passed without loss to whatever progress the patient has made. This is especially true for people who have undergone behavior therapy while taking the medication. Patients for whom drug therapy works say that their symptoms become less intense. They may still get an occasional obsessive thought, but they no longer feel they must act on it, and rather than staying in their minds, the thought goes away.

Other Drug Treatment Strategies for OCD

When anti-obsessive drugs fail to work against OCD, other drug treatment options are available. One of these is to combine different anti-obsessive medications. This approach helps some people who get no relief from clomipramine, for example, unless it is combined with fluoxetine. Another tactic is to combine the use of an anti-obsessive drug with other medications that enhance its effects. One such medication is L-tryptophan, a substance from which serotonin is produced naturally in the body.

Other medications that have been shown to augment the effectiveness of anti-obsessive drugs in some cases of OCD are lithium, fenfluarmine, and buspirone. Two antipsychotic drugs—haloperidol and pimozide—are also said to have benefited a small number of patients who either have tics or a psychological syndrome called schizotypal personality disorder. All of these augmentation strategies are, however, unproven and still being carefully investigated.

Additionally, a small number of people—most of whom have depression as their primary symptom, with OCD as a secondary effect of this depression—are helped by antidepressant drugs that do not enhance serotonin transmission. In such cases, relieving the depression results in reduction of obsessions and compulsions.

Psychosurgery

The term *psychosurgery* refers to surgery performed on the brain to relieve symptoms of a mental disorder. Until the 1950's, such surgery was used to treat the most severe cases of OCD and some other mental disorders as well. However, the misuse of psychosurgery and the danger it posed to the safety of the patient gave it an extremely bad reputation.

Recently, however, improvements in surgical technique have made psychosurgery much safer, explains John Greist, with the result that it has found a place in the treatment of rare and very severe cases of OCD that resist drugs, behavior therapy, and all other treatments. This surgery involves cutting the neural connections between the frontal and deeper parts of the brain, in effect preventing transmission of messages from those parts of the brain involved in obsessions and compulsions.

At the opposite pole from those patients whose OCD is so severe as to require surgery are persons who have been able to control their symptoms through behavior therapy alone, as will be seen in chapter 7.

CHAPTER 7
BEHAVIOR THERAPY AND PSYCHOTHERAPY

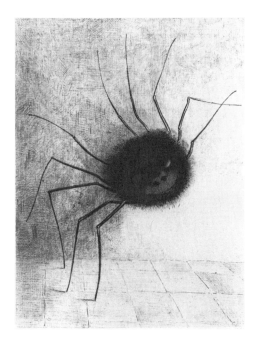

Behavior therapy for OCD involves the patient's gradual exposure to the objects or events he or she most fears.

Despite the severity of her obsessions, Lizzie, the 11-year-old girl described in chapter 3, whose prayers and checking rituals were intended to prevent harm from coming to her mother, never needed to take anti-obsessive drugs. With the help of her therapist she was able to eliminate her checking, her prayers, and another obsession—a fear of mud—through behavior therapy. This therapy involved techniques called *exposure* and *response prevention.*

As a first step in this therapy, Lizzie and her therapist, Andrea Gitow, created a hierarchy of the objects, thoughts, and situations that Lizzie feared, rating them according to how much anxiety each produced. Beginning with the least fearsome items, the therapist then exposed Lizzie to each threatening object, thought, or situation, while simultaneously preventing her from engaging in her rituals. This eventually reduced and finally eliminated—extinguished, in behavioral therapy terms—her anxiety in each threatening situation.

They began with a bit of mud on a table in front of Lizzie. She touched it, at first gingerly with her index finger until her anxiety in doing so was gone. She also had a "homework" assignment to practice for two hours a day whatever she had done in her treatment session. Her mother helped her keep a record of how much anxiety she felt in each situation as she repeated it.

To extinguish Lizzie's praying rituals, the therapist asked Lizzie to try to avoid ritualizing when her fears came up, but to instead focus on her anxiety and run it through her mind while talking about it. She was also given alternative, more adaptive ways to respond to her anxiety, such as sitting down and writing what she felt, drawing her "scary" feelings, and telling her grandmother that she was scared. Gradually her anxiety lessened, and finally it disappeared completely, to the point where her therapist was able to come to her home and have mud fights with her in the backyard.

Principles of Behavior Therapy

As described in chapter 5, behavioral therapy for OCD is based on learning theory. It is effective because even though the basis of OCD is biological, a person's response to the factors that provoke it is learned and can be changed. With repeated exposure to such factors, and the practice of response prevention under controlled conditions, the affected individual eventually learns that nothing bad happens if he or she does not perform rituals in response to an anxiety-provoking stimulus. As the anxiety decreases, the rituals are no longer needed and fall away.

Victims of OCD who deliberately expose themselves to a fear-provoking stimulus while forcing themselves not to perform their rituals, as described in chapter 4, are actually practicing a form of behavior therapy.

Stages of Behavioral Therapy

The most widely used behavior therapy program for adults with OCD has three stages. Stage 1 consists of collecting information about the patient's OCD, describing the nature of the treatment, and establishing a treatment plan based on the patient's least and most anxiety-provoking stimuli, as described earlier.

Stage 2 consists of the treatment sessions themselves. These may be held as often as every weekday or, if not, at least three times a week. Patients are first exposed to their least feared stimulus by imagining it, and then by having it actually present. This procedure is then repeated for stimuli that produce stronger anxiety.

During stage 2, the patient is asked to completely refrain from performing any rituals and to avoid experiencing any relief from the anxiety that results from this restraint. The objective of this is to have the patient learn to tolerate his or her anxiety. Many persons who enter into behavioral therapy need to be highly motivated in order to tolerate the anxiety resulting from such drastic measures, but for most the decrease in anxiety that comes with each therapy session provides a strong reinforcement to continue.

Stage 3 begins after the patient's obsessions and compulsions have been eliminated. This stage involves setting up a "maintenance regime" to enable the patient to preserve his or her achievements and prevent the reappearance of obsessive thoughts and rituals. This may require weekly sessions for weeks or months as the patient learns new patterns of behavior to replace the abandoned rituals.

The purpose of behavior therapy for OCD is not only to stop the symptoms of the disorder but to provide the individual with a set of techniques she or he can use whenever stress or some other factor brings on a recurrence of OCD. People learn how to expose themselves

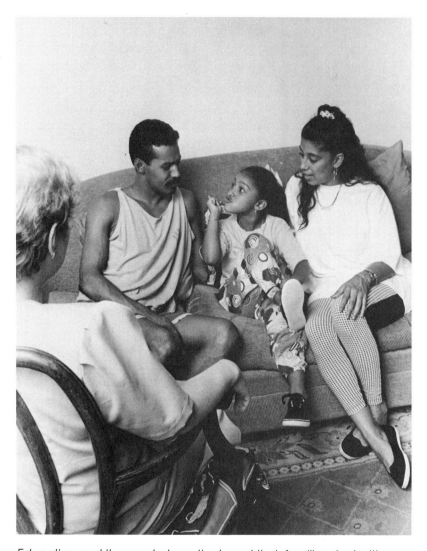

Education and therapy help patients and their families deal with obsessive-compulsive disorder in an enlightened and constructive manner.

to what they fear and thereby decrease their anxiety and avoid compulsive rituals. This permits most people who have had behavior therapy to maintain their achievements for a long time and to cope with new outbreaks of OCD.

Imaginal Forms of Behavior Therapy

Another way of conquering feared thoughts in OCD involves using the imagination. In this type of therapy, the patient with OCD is exposed to the thought by telling or writing a story about what would happen if a family member for whom the patient has fears should actually die. The patient is asked to imagine this experience in detail, including the clothes being worn by the family member, the setting in which the death occurs, and so on.

Imaginal therapy exposes persons with OCD to their underlying fears by asking them to describe what would happen if these fears were realized. The therapist makes a tape of this description as the patient speaks and then plays it back to the patient until he or she becomes used to the anxiety expressed in the story.

As the patient tells the story, the therapist makes an audiotape of it and plays this back to the patient until he or she becomes used to the anxiety expressed in the story, while at the same time making a conscious commitment not to perform the associated ritual. The therapist at the same time also provides "coping statements" for the patient to repeat, such as "Stay with this, my anxiety will eventually go down," when the anxiety is strong.

Sam, the boy described in chapter 3 who feared that he was gay and would commit suicide, was treated behaviorally. He agreed to stop asking his family for reassurance about his fears, and his family was instructed to stop reinforcing his fears by refusing to answer any questions he asked about them.

Part of his therapy involved listening to recorded tapes designed to extinguish his anxieties. One such tape told him that he was gay and might as well admit it, another stated that he had an unknown emotional disorder and would never get well, and so on. Each tape lasted two to three minutes, and Sam listened to each one about six times a day. The tapes changed as his treatment progressed. Gradually the ideas expressed on the tapes lost their power to make him anxious. During his behavior therapy, he also took clomipramine, which he continued to take in a maintenance dose after the behavior therapy ended.

In yet another form of imaginal therapy known as *thought stopping*, the patient administers some kind of negative stimulus to him- or herself in response to an obsessive thought. The stimulus may be as simple as snapping a rubber band worn around the wrist whenever an obsession arises.

Treating Children

The behavioral treatment of children with OCD is essentially the same as that for adults, although some aspects of the therapy may have to be modified. One problem with behavior therapy for children is that very young children may not be able to accurately report changes in their behavior during the course of the therapy. Another is that children do not come for treatment on their own but are brought by the parents. The therapist must then determine whether the parents are overreacting to the child's behavior—or even unconsciously seeking therapy themselves.

For younger children, a reward system is built into behavior therapy to help motivate them to stick to it. This system may involve listing desirable behaviors and giving a prize or reward for achieving these behaviors.

Teaching Families To Support Behavior Therapy

According to Barbara Livingston and Steven Rasmussen, positive family relationships and the feeling on the part of the patient that he or she is understood greatly enhance the benefits of behavior therapy, medication, and other treatments for OCD. Because of this, part of the treatment for OCD involves teaching the patients' relatives ways to support them as they work to control their symptoms.

Behavioral family therapists, for example, help families to improve their internal relationships and reduce conflict, making it easier for the OCD patient to let go of symptoms and easier for the rest of the family to live with the patient. A behavior therapy "contract," negotiated between the patient and the other members of the family, may help. The contract lists specific goals toward which the patient intends to work and describes specific ways in which other family members will help the patient to do this.

Thus, the patient with a contamination obsession, who has avoided touching dirty clothing, may be helped to sort and launder his or her clothing by family members who agree to keep the patient company while he or she is doing the wash. The family may also offer a specific reward when the job is completed, such as going out to dinner. The behavior therapy contract also spells out a negative consequence, such as putting the dirty clothes back in the patient's room, if the job is not done. The patient must agree beforehand to all of these rules.

Support-group therapy is a useful form of treatment for obsessive-compulsive disorder. Directed by a therapist, the group may be composed of children, adolescents, or adults, or of several families with members who have the disorder. It is helpful for those who have the disorder to understand that they are not the only persons it affects.

The question of reassurance is an important one. As Dr. Greist explains, withholding the reassurance that persons with OCD so often seek actually helps them through the process of behavior therapy, since this process requires that they be exposed to their anxiety rather than avoid it. However, the withholding must be done with the right attitude, using a neutral tone and avoiding harshness or sarcasm.

Those who treat OCD also counsel families to expect its symptoms to flare up during times of stress for the patient, but encourage them to give praise and recognition to the patient throughout such periods, even for such small improvements as taking a shower that lasts a few minutes less than usual.

Effectiveness of Behavior Therapy

If they work diligently at their treatment program, says Dr. Greist, from 60% to 90% of OCD patients will benefit from behavior therapy, with a 50% to 80% reduction in their symptoms. Further treatment, however, may be needed before improvement becomes apparent. Nevertheless, there are some persons with OCD who do not respond to behavior therapy.

Although the reasons for this are not fully clear, severe depression is one factor that decreases the effectiveness of such therapy. Certain drugs will decrease its effectiveness, since the learning that occurs while under the influence of these drugs does not remain after the drug treatment is stopped.

Behavior Therapy or Anti-Obsessive Drugs?

Some persons with OCD choose behavior therapy because they do not want the side effects of drugs or are concerned about the negative consequences that may result from the use of such drugs over many years. This is especially a consideration with children who have OCD and face a lifetime of medication.

Other persons choose to begin their treatment with behavior therapy to see how far they can go with this, sometimes finding that they are able to avoid drugs altogether. Still others begin with drug therapy to obtain some relief from their symptoms and then start behavior therapy. This is true for some adults who have chronic OCD and multiple rituals and obsessions or intense obsessions that interfere with their functioning. By contrast, some persons choose drug therapy because they are reluctant to face the anxiety involved in behavior therapy or to make the effort it requires. Many persons with OCD begin both forms of treatment at the same time.

In the case of teenagers and children, Penzel says that he attempts to work first without medications. If it then becomes clear that despite his best efforts, the child's anxieties, obsessions, or compulsions are so severe that they prevent him or her from following instructions, he refers the child to a psychiatrist for medication.

Milder cases, with fairly specific and contained rituals, are usually treated first with behavior therapy, in the hope that the patients will get used to experiencing anxiety and learn alternative ways of managing it without the need for medication.

Cognitive Therapy

Cognitive therapy focuses on illogical or irrational thinking. Although there is little documented evidence of its effectiveness for OCD, some therapists begin using it after behavioral therapy has gone on for some time.

Rational-emotive therapy (RET), a type of cognitive therapy, teaches people that it is not external objects or other people who disturb them, but rather it is they who disturb themselves through their own illogical thinking. As a first step, this therapy involves teaching patients what constitutes illogical and irrational thought and then showing them how to challenge and change such thought patterns to make them logical.

For persons who tell themselves, "I should always do everything perfectly" or "I must get everybody's love and approval at all times," explains Pensel, he teaches ways of changing these statements into others such as, "I'd like to do everything as well as I can, but I accept the fact that nobody is perfect" or "It would be nice to get everybody's love and approval, but that's not possible, you can't please everybody."

Essentially, says Penzel, RET shows people that in this universe "we can only control ourselves; we cannot control other people or the world."

Uses of Psychotherapy

Although it has not been as effective as behavior therapy or the use of anti-obsessive drugs, psychotherapy can be of use in treating OCD by providing support for patients and dealing with problems that exist between the patient's parents and the patient, between the parents and the patient's children, and between the patient and his or her siblings.

With regard to support for the patient, the changes that accompany the extinction of obsessions and rituals may leave many "gaps" of open time during the day. "It's very frightening to suddenly have eight hours free that you used to spend washing," explains researcher Andrea Gitow. The stress that comes with this change, she says, may send the patient back to the behavior he or she is familiar with.

In particular, adolescents who have spent a great deal of time ritualizing instead of socializing may lack social skills already acquired by their friends. If they recover from their OCD, they often find themselves afraid of new relationships. Psychotherapy can help them to learn decision-making and problem-solving skills as well as other ways in which to reenter a normal life.

One useful form of psychotherapy is the support group. Such a group is run by a therapist and may include several families with members who have OCD or may instead consist of adults, children, or teenagers in various stages of recovery. Since OCD is so often a hidden disorder, it is very helpful for its victims to realize they are not the only ones who have it.

Psychotherapy can also provide useful insights for people whose OCD appears to be related to emotional issues. Such was the case for the teenager described in chapter 4 who was obsessed by the fear that a piece of molding would fall from a building and hit him. By the time he was 22, his obsessions had spread to fears of other dangers and produced checking rituals that isolated him from other people.

Working with his therapist, this young man came to the realization that he had not finished mourning his father's death and that he was afraid of his anger at his mother, who had struggled to support him.

These two deeply buried problems seemed to lie at the core of his obsessive-compulsive behavior. As his therapy gradually proved to him that his anger was not dangerous, his obsessions disappeared.

The Prognosis for Persons with OCD

Unfortunately, although OCD can be controlled, it does not seem in most cases to ever fully disappear. According to Drs. Susan Swedo and Judith Rapoport, most studies have found OCD to be chronic, with half of all patients remaining unchanged and often left with moderate disability, social isolation, and celibacy.

As Livingston and Rasmussen point out, "Most patients with OCD have a waxing and waning course," which means that symptoms are likely to recur, especially during times of change or stress. Nevertheless, continuing research, as well as the refinement and increasingly effective use of behavior therapy, will help those affected by OCD to live increasingly productive lives while coping effectively with the disorder.

CHAPTER 8

WHO HAS OCD?

The compulsive personality, in contrast to the individual with obsessive-compulsive disorder, tends to be highly satisfied with him- or herself, insisting that others change their behavior to follow his or her lead.

Many of the compulsions and obsessions of OCD resemble "normal," commonplace behaviors and beliefs. Many people, for example, occasionally experience numbers or music running through their heads, bite their nails, or habitually "knock wood." Others are rigid in their habits, always punctual and excessively neat, and insist on "everything in its place." Young children have many rituals, ranging from the demand for a nightly bedtime story to avoiding cracks in the sidewalk when they walk. Where, then, should the line be drawn between these types of behaviors and OCD?

Observing that all persons have fleeting obsessions and compulsions and that, like childhood superstitions, they are "normal and natural," Gitow explains that they constitute a disorder only when they are so distressing or time consuming that they interfere with an individual's life.

Another criterion for recognizing OCD is that the obsessive thoughts are intense, distressing, and accompanied by a belief in great harm or sorrow if the ensuing ritual is not performed. The diagnosis of OCD is based on the extent to which such a thought lingers in the mind and the intensity of the anxiety related to the thought. The person with OCD cannot simply step on a crack in the sidewalk and forget about it. The following sections describe the distinction between familiar normal behaviors, OCD, and other psychiatric disorders.

Childhood Rituals and Superstitions

According to psychiatrist Henrietta L. Leonard of the NIMH, rituals and superstitions are normal in young children. At about two and a half years of age, they demand routines during meals and baths. Later they insist on bedtime rituals. At around ages five or six, children begin to perform rituals in groups, playing games like jump rope or jacks, which have many rules. At about seven, they begin to collect objects such as baseball cards.

Dr. Leonard believes that the symptoms of OCD are not simply extreme versions of these childhood behaviors or others, such as the idea that walking under a ladder brings bad luck or that finding a four-leaf clover brings good luck, as some experts previously thought. She points out first that normal rituals end by about eight years of age, whereas OCD often begins around seven but can also begin during adolescence and even later. Second, says Dr. Leonard, normal rituals assist the child's healthy development by helping him or her to deal with anxiety and by enhancing the child's social development, whereas the rituals of OCD have the opposite effect, preventing the child from functioning well, isolating him or her socially, and involving great pain and unhappiness.

What is more, observes Leonard, children with OCD know there is a difference in their behavior.

Compulsive Personality Disorder

Despite our having observed in chapter 1 that they differ from persons with OCD, those immaculately neat people that we loosely call "compulsive" may in fact—if their traits are sufficiently severe—have a compulsive personality disorder. This type of personality, while not afflicted with OCD, insists on doing everything in his or her own way and is obstinate, often ungenerous, and unable to relax and enjoy life. One major difference between the compulsive personality and the individual with OCD is that compulsive personalities, far from being unhappy about their behavior, are instead dissatisfied with everyone else. In contrast to the victims of OCD, who desperately want to change, the compulsive personality is satisfied with him- or herself and wants others to become more like them. Nevertheless, it remains difficult to determine where the obsessions of everyday life leave off and OCD begins.

Phobias

A *phobia* is an exaggerated, irrational fear of a certain object or type of object or situation. Phobic personalities resemble those with OCD in that both have excessive fears and try to avoid feared objects, while recognizing that their feelings and behavior are illogical.

However, there are differences that enable psychiatrists to distinguish between phobic disorder and OCD. Whereas phobic personalities are generally most disturbed by actual contact with the object of their fear, persons with OCD are more troubled by the prospect of the lengthy rituals they will have to perform as a result of the contact.

Rather than being self-satisfied, as is the compulsive personality, the individual affected by OCD is tormented by his or her obsessions and ritualized compulsions and desperately seeks to be rid of them.

Another difference is that persons with obsessive-compulsive disorder are likely to feel disgust more than anxiety when faced with their feared objects, while phobic personalities feel more fear or anxiety. Finally, the phobic's fears are more likely to be focused on something quite specific that he or she can fairly easily avoid, whereas the person with OCD can never entirely escape his or her obsession, and many different situations can set off the rituals intended to negate its effects.

Depression

Persons with OCD almost always also have depression, often brought on by having to spend many hours doing rituals. OCD with depression as a secondary problem can be difficult to distinguish from depression as a primary problem, since many persons with primary depression also develop obsessions, often in the form of repeated self-condemning thoughts.

Generally, obsessions related to depression tend to focus on the past, whereas the obsessions of OCD more often relate to fears about the future. Another distinction is that persons with OCD try to resist their obsessions, whereas those who are depressed rarely do so.

When depression is a primary problem, obsessions and compulsions go away when the depression is successfully treated.

Schizophrenia

Schizophrenia is a psychotic disorder characterized, among other things, by delusions (for example, of being poisoned) that may be difficult to distinguish from the contamination obsessions of OCD. However, the vast majority of persons with OCD are, except for their specific obsessions and rituals, otherwise psychologically normal, and as has been said, they resist their obsessions and recognize that these ideas are created by their own minds. A schizophrenic, by contrast, would insist that she or he really was being poisoned by some external power.

Symptoms of depression are commonly found in people who suffer from obsessive-compulsive disorder, complicating diagnosis. The depression will usually disappear if the compulsive behavior is successfully treated.

There are other differences that distinguish schizophrenia from OCD. Schizophrenics often experience hallucinations, whereas people with OCD do not. Furthermore, persons with OCD can have close, loving relationships, whereas those with schizophrenia generally cannot.

Diagnosis of OCD

To determine whether someone has OCD, psychiatrists use a combination of measures. According to Andrea Gitow, diagnosis, or assessment, as it is also called, "is very important and must be thorough,

Although it may be difficult to distinguish the delusions of schizophrenia from the compulsions about contamination and dirt that are common in OCD, persons with schizophrenia, such as those shown in this late-19th-century French psychiatric ward, believe that they are in fact being victimized by an external person or power. By contrast, the vast majority of persons with OCD recognize that they are affected with a disorder.

because the meaning of the same ritual might be entirely different for different people. One person might wash because he fears contamination on his hands will make him sick, while another washes because she thinks that if she doesn't a plane will crash over Chicago."

Diagnostic tests include lists on which the patient checks off his or her own symptoms, rating scales used by the examiner who observes the patient's behavior and rates the severity of each item on a list of symptoms, and structured interviews in which an examiner asks specific questions from a questionnaire. Each question or item on a scale is scored according to its severity, and the total score indicates whether the person is likely to have OCD and, if so, the severity of the case. Another form of assessment is a diary kept by the person with OCD symptoms that records all obsessions and rituals performed during one week.

The *Yale-Brown Obsessive-Compulsive Scale* is a frequently used scale that rates the severity of obsessions and compulsions. It consists of two parts and comes in different versions for children and adults. The first part is a checklist of all possible symptoms that allows the examiner to discover which ones the patient has. The second part is a series of 19 questions asked by an interviewer. This is used to determine how much time is taken up by obsessions and compulsions, how much they interfere with daily life, how much distress they cause, how much control the person has over them, and how much the patient resists them. This scale also enables the examiner to assess how much insight the patient has into his or her symptoms and the general severity of the OCD.

Another test is the *Leyton Obsessional Inventory*. It involves sorting cards according to whether or not the person has the symptom printed on each card. The test covers 44 symptoms such as checking, cleanliness, order, and persistent thoughts. The cards to which the patient has said yes are then further rated ccording to the degree to which she or he resists having each symptom and the extent to which the symptom interferes with daily activity.

Whatever the scores obtained on such tests, it is important to remember that, as Greist says, they "are only indicators of the possibility of obsessive-compulsive disorder." Even though someone has obvious symptoms, further assessment is needed to make sure that OCD is what is causing them—not another condition such as depression or anxiety.

What is more, no matter what the symptoms, in the end the decision whether to follow through with treatment depends on the overall effect of the symptoms on the life of the person in question. "No list of symptoms can take the place of common sense," writes Rapoport in *The Boy Who Couldn't Stop Washing*. "If someone is living their life in psychological comfort, and their habits do not disrupt their work or their personal lives, then it does not matter what their 'score' is on any scale—they do not have OCD."

On the other hand, someone who is experiencing real suffering and disruption of his or her life—even from just a single symptom, such as washing—would probably want to consult a psychologist or psychiatrist. A list of sources of help appears in the appendix. With awareness and understanding of OCD growing among both scientists and the general public, the days when people with this disorder felt they had to suffer in silence are at last over.

APPENDIX

APPENDIX:
FOR MORE INFORMATION

The following sources can provide more information about OCD and its treatment, as well as names of therapists, clinics, self-help groups, and support groups in different parts of the country.

General Information

Canadian Mental Health Association
2160 Yonge Street
3rd Floor
Toronto, Ontario M4F 2Z3
(416) 484-7750

Child and Adolescent OCD Treatment
    Study
Anxiety Disorders Clinic
New York State Psychiatric Institute at
    Columbia University
722 West 168th Street
New York, NY 10032
(212) 960-5627

National Institute of Mental Health
Office of Scientific Information
Room 15C-05
5600 Fishers Lane
Rockville, MD 20857
(301) 443-4513

National Mental Health Association
1021 Prince Street

Alexandria, VA 22314
(800) 969-NMHA
(703) 684-7722

The Obsessive-Compulsive Foundation
P.O. Box 9573
New Haven, CT 06535
(203) 772-0565
(203) 498-8476 (fax)

Obsessive Compulsive Information
    Center
Department of Psychiatry
University of Wisconsin
Center for Health Sciences
600 Highland Avenue
Madison, WI 53792
(608) 263-6171

Anxiety Disorders

Anxiety Disorders Association of
    America
6000 Executive Blvd., Suite 200
Rockville, MD 20852

Anxiety Disorders Center
Department of Psychiatry
University of Wisconsin Center for
    Health Sciences
600 Highland Avenue
Madison, WI 53792
(608) 263-6056

Behavior Therapy

Association for Advancement of
    Behavior Therapy
15 West 36th Street
New York, NY 10018
(212) 279-7970

FURTHER READING

Berg, Carol Zaremba, Judith L. Rapoport, and Richard P. Wolff. "Behavioral Treatment of Obsessive Compulsive Disorder in Childhood." In *Obsessive-Compulsive Disorder in Children and Adolescents*, edited by Judith L. Rapoport. Washington, DC: American Psychiatric Press, 1989.

Clarizio, Harvey F. "Obsessive-Compulsive Disorder: The Secretive Syndrome." *Psychology in the Schools* 28 (1991): 106–115.

Flament, Martine F., Elisabeth Koby, Judith L. Rapoport, et al. "Childhood Obsessive-Compulsive Disorder: A Prospective Follow-Up Study." *Journal of Child and Adolescent Psychiatry* 31 (1990): 363–80.

Freud, Sigmund. "Notes upon a Case of Obsessional Neurosis." In *Three Case Histories*, edited and introduced by Philip Rieff. New York: Collier, 1963.

Greist, John H. *Obsessive Compulsive Disorder: A Guide.* Madison, WI: Board of Regents of the University of Wisconsin System (Obsessive Compulsive Information Center), 1991.

Hollander, Eric, Michael R. Liebowitz, and Jack M. Gorman. "Anxiety Disorders." In *The American Psychiatric Press Textbook of Psychiatry*, edited by John A. Talbott, Robert E. Hales, and Stuart C. Yudofsky. Washington, DC: American Psychiatric Press, 1988.

Insel, Thomas R. "Obsessive-Compulsive Disorder: The Clinical Picture." In *New Findings in Obsessive-Compulsive Disorder*, edited by Thomas R. Insel. Washington, DC: American Psychiatric Press, 1984.

Jenike, Michael A. "Controlled Trial of Fluvoxamine in Obsessive-Compulsive Disorder." *American Journal of Psychiatry* 147 (1990): 1209–15.

Lenane, Marge. "Families and Obsessive-Compulsive Disorder." In *Obsessive-Compulsive Disorder in Children and Adolescents*, edited by Judith L. Rapoport. Washington, DC: American Psychiatric Press, 1989.

Leonard, Henrietta L. "Childhood Rituals and Superstitions: Developmental and Cultural Perspective." In *Obsessive-Compulsive Disorder in Children and Adolescents*, edited by Judith L. Rapoport. Washington, DC: American Psychiatric Press, 1989.

Leonard, Henrietta L., Erica L. Goldberger, Judith L. Rapoport, Deborah L. Cheslow, and Susan E. Swedo. "Childhood Rituals: Normal Development or Obsessive-Compulsive Symptoms?" *Journal of the American Academy of Child and Adolescent Psychiatry* 29 (1990): 17-23.

Livingston, Barbara, and Steven Rasmussen. *Learning to Live with OCD*. New Haven, CT: OC Foundation, 1989.

McDougle, Christopher, et al. "Pathophysiology of Obsessive-Compulsive Disorder." *American Journal of Psychiatry* 146 (1989): 1350–51.

Nemiah, John C. "Obsessive-Compulsive Disorder (Obsessive-Compulsive Neurosis)." In *Comprehensive Textbook of Psychiatry*, edited by Harold I. Kaplan and Benjamin J. Sadock. 4th ed. Baltimore and London: Williams and Wilkins, 1985.

Pasnau, Robert O. "The Anxiety Disorders." In *Diagnosis and Treatment of Anxiety Disorders*, edited by Robert O. Pasnau. Washington, DC: American Psychiatric Press, 1984.

Penzel, Frederick I. "Obsessive-Compulsive Disorders in Children: A Little-Known Problem." *Long Island Parent* 3 (1989): 11.

Pleasants, Carol N. *Trichotillomania* (pamphlet). New Haven, CT: OC Foundation, 1990.

Rapoport, Judith L. *The Boy Who Couldn't Stop Washing: The Experience and Treatment of Obsessive-Compulsive Disorder*. New York: New American Library, 1990.

———. "The Neurobiology of Obsessive-Compulsive Disorder." *Journal of the American Medical Association* 260 (1988): 2888–90.

Rasmussen, Steven A., and Ming T. Tsuang. "DSM-III Obsessive-Compulsive Disorder: Clinical Characteristics and Family History." *American Journal of Psychiatry* 143 (1986): 317–22.

Swedo, Susan E., and Judith L. Rapoport. "Phenomenology and Differential Diagnosis of Obsessive-Compulsive Disorder in Children and Adolescents." In *Obsessive-Compulsive Disorder in Children and Adolescents*, edited by Judith L. Rapoport. Washington, DC: American Psychiatric Press, 1989.

GLOSSARY

antidepressant a drug that prevents or relieves depression; three drugs developed as antidepressants have also proven effective for OCD

anti-obsessive one of three antidepressant drugs (clomipramine, fluoxetine, and fluvoxamine) that have been found to relieve the obsessions and compulsions of OCD

anxiety an overwhelming sense of apprehension caused by tension or distress; fear without an identifiable object to be feared

basal ganglia structures deep within the brain that relay messages between the front part of the brain and the lower motor and sensory areas

behavior therapy a form of therapy for OCD that involves exposing the patient to an anxiety-provoking stimulus while preventing the patient from performing a ritual in response to the stimulus

chorea any of various nervous disorders characterized by involuntary movements of the body, face, and limbs

clomipramine a strong antidepressant drug that affects serotonin levels; sometimes used to treat patients with obsessions and compulsions

cognitive therapy a form of therapy for OCD that focuses on changing illogical or irrational thoughts so as to make them more logical, with the goal of eliminating incorrect ideas that may lead to obsessions and rituals

compulsion the urge to perform a certain behavior in response to an obsession

compulsive personality a type of personality that is rigid, perfectionistic, neat, punctual, obstinate, emotionally cold, and critical of others; it differs from obsessive-compulsive disorder

delusion a false belief regarding the self or people or things outside the self, firmly held despite all evidence to the contrary

depression a psychological disorder characterized by dejection and hopelessness, inactivity, poor sleep, weight loss, and preoccupation with feelings of guilt and delusions involving a particular part of the body

epilepsy any of various disorders marked by disturbed electrical rhythms and spontaneous firing of neurons in the central nervous system; typically takes the form of convulsive attacks

etiology the cause(s) or origin of a disease

fluoxetine a strong antidepressant drug that affects the concentrations of serotonin at nerve endings; used to treat patients with depression

fluvoxamine a strong antidepressant drug that is used in most European countries but has not been approved for use in the United States

learning theory a theory that describes how knowledge is acquired and then modified as new learning occurs; it is used both to describe how the rituals of OCD are acquired and how behavior therapy can enable the individual affected by OCD to learn new responses to the stimuli that trigger his or her anxieties

Leyton Obsessional Inventory a system that ranks the severity of 44 symptoms to indicate the amount of time an individual with OCD devotes to obsessions and compulsions

metabolism the sum total of the chemical processes taking place within the body that enable an organism to grow and develop and which make energy available for its use

neuron or nerve cell a cell of the nervous system that conducts impulses and makes up part of the brain, the spinal cord, or a nerve

neurotransmitter any of the chemicals that mediate the transmission of a nerve impulse across the synapse, or gap, between adjacent neurons, or nerve cells

obsession a persistent idea, thought, image, or impulse that is intrusive and senseless, often resulting in compulsive behavior

obsessive-compulsive disorder (OCD) a psychological illness that usually includes uncontrollable obsessive thoughts as well as compulsive behavior

phobia an exaggerated, irrational fear of a certain object or situation

positron emission tomography (PET) an imaging technique that produces a cross-sectional view of the physical and chemical activity in a specific organ of the body, making possible the recognition of various substances and their participation in that activity

psychoanalytic theory a body of ideas developed by Sigmund Freud, based on the premise that repressed feelings of anger, fear, and guilt underlie most psychological disorders

psychosurgery cerebral surgery used in treating psychic symptoms

psychotherapy any of a number of systematic procedures designed to change maladaptive behavior and help patients live more positive and fulfilling lives; it includes such therapies as psychoanalysis, group therapy, and behavioral therapy

rational-emotive therapy (RET) therapy emphasizing rationality and self-sufficiency over emotionalism and self-indulgence

ritual a pattern of behavior that reduces the anxiety created by an obsession

schizophrenia a group of related mental disorders in which a person loses touch with reality; characterized by profound emotional withdrawal and bizarre behavior, often including delusions and hallucinations

serotonin a neurotransmitter substance thought to transmit messages that inhibit impulsiveness, aggression, anxiety, suicidal tendencies, and learning. An abnormality in the amount of serotonin present in the brain is thought to be a factor in the etiology of OCD

serotonin reuptake inhibitor a drug that prevents neurons that have released a neurotransmitter from reabsorbing it, thus leaving more of this neurotransmitter available for transmitting messages to the receiving neurons

somatic obsessions worries about one's body that may provoke the need for constant checking to assure oneself of being physically all right

Sydenham's chorea a chorea, or series of movements, that occurs in many cases of rheumatic fever and in certain other infections; it usually effects children and adolescents

synapse a tiny gap between neurons, across which messages are carried by neurotransmitters

tic an uncontrollable, rapid, repetitive muscle movement or vocalization (sound)

Tourette's syndrome a rare disease defined by involuntary tics and verbalizations

trichotillomania a disease characterized by the action of pulling out one's hair in order to relieve anxiety

Yale-Brown Obsessive-Compulsive Scale a frequently used scale, composed of a checklist of symptoms and 19 questions, that determines the extent to which certain obsessions and compulsions interfere with one's life

INDEX

PICTURE CREDITS

Richard Sebastian was born in Queens, New York, where he received his primary and secondary education. After graduating from Queens College with a bachelor of arts degree in English literature, he attended Hofstra University, receiving a master of arts degree in psychology. While working in clinical psychology at a number of health care institutions, he began to write professionally in his field, and during the past 15 years he has written journal articles, book chapters, and other materials concerning various aspects of psychology and mental health for both professional and general readers.

Solomon H. Snyder, M.D., is Distinguished Service Professor of Neuroscience, Pharmacology, and Psychiatry and director of the Department of Neuroscience at the Johns Hopkins University School of Medicine. He has served as president of the Society for Neuroscience and in 1978 received the Albert Lasker Award in Medical Research for his discovery of opiate receptors in the brain. Dr. Snyder is a member of the National Academy of Sciences and a Fellow of the American Academy of Arts and Sciences. He is the author of *Drugs and the Brain*, *Uses of Marijuana*, *Madness and the Brain*, *The Troubled Mind*, and *Biological Aspects of Mental Disorder*. He is also the general editor of Chelsea House's ENCYCLOPEDIA OF PSYCHOACTIVE DRUGS.

C. Everett Koop, M.D., Sc.D., is former Surgeon General, deputy assistant secretary for health, and director of the Office of International Health of the U.S. Public Health Service. A pediatric surgeon with an international reputation, he was previously surgeon-in-chief of Children's Hospital of Philadelphia and professor of pediatric surgery and pediatrics at the University of Pennsylvania. Dr. Koop is the author of more than 175 articles and books on the practice of medicine. He has served as surgery editor of the *Journal of Clinical Pediatrics* and editor-in-chief of the *Journal of Pediatric Surgery*. Dr. Koop has received nine honorary degrees and numerous other awards, including the Denis Brown Gold Medal of the British Association of Paediatric Surgeons, the William E. Ladd Gold Medal of the American Academy of Pediatrics, and the Copernicus Medal of the Surgical Society of Poland. He is a chevalier of the French Legion of Honor and a member of the Royal College of Surgeons, London.